THE BOOK OF

Light

PASTA SAUCES

THE BOOK OF

Light

PASTA SAUCES

ANNE SHEASBY

Photographed by
SIMON BUTCHER

HPBooks

ANOTHER BEST SELLING VOLUME FROM HP BOOKS

HPBooks
Published by The Berkley Publishing Group
200 Madison Avenue
New York, NY 10016

9 8 7 6 5 4 3 2 1

ISBN 1-55788-207-X

By arrangement with Salamander Books Ltd.

Home Economist: Justine Dickenson
Printed in Belgium by Proost International Book Production

CONTENTS

INTRODUCTION

Pasta was once thought to be high in calories and therefore a 'fattening' food to be avoided. Nothing could be further from the truth. Pasta is, in fact, a highly nutritious food - it is an excellent source of carbohydrate and provides protein, dietary fiber, vitamins and minerals. It is low in fat and is a valuable source of energy.

The sauces served with pasta are usually responsible for piling on fat and calories, but with careful selection of ingredients, and replacing the more traditional ones, such as cream and butter, with lighter alternatives, you'll be able to create healthful, delicious pasta sauces that are low in fat and calories.

The Book of Light Pasta Sauces gives recipes for sauces made with meat, poultry, fish and shellfish, vegetables, and eggs and cheese, all illustrated in full color, with step-by-step instructions and calorie and fat levels for quick, easy reference.

——COOKING WITH PASTA——

Pasta is traditionally associated with Italy and has played an important role in the Italian diet for centuries. Yet egg and rice noodles also form a part of the staple diet of many Asian countries and some people believe pasta actually originated in China. Today, however, pasta is a popular food all over the world, and the range of fresh and dried pastas that are now available in supermarkets and speciality food stores is considerable.

VARIETIES OF PASTA

The word pasta literally means 'dough' and this dough is a basic mixture of wheat flour and water, to which flavorings and colorings are often added. Most dried pasta is a pale yellow color. Pasta which has eggs added to the basic mixture is a darker yellow and is known as *pasta all'uova*. *Pasta verde* is flavored with spinach to give it a green color; *pasta rossa* has tomato puree added to make it a pale reddish orange. Other, less common, colors of pasta available include black (colored with squid ink), pale brown (flavored with chocolate or mushrooms), deep pink (colored with beets), and deep yellow (colored with saffron). The darker brown varieties of whole-wheat and buckwheat pasta contain more fiber than the other types of pasta and have a chewier texture. Filled pastas, such as ravioli and tortellini, traditionally contain stuffings of ground meats or a classic mixture of spinach and cheese.

Homemade pasta is becoming more popular and is relatively easy to make, particularly with the help of a pasta-making machine, which both kneads and rolls the dough for you. Homemade pasta is made from a simple mixture of flour, salt, oil and water or eggs. The best flour to use is semolina flour but this is quite difficult to obtain, so bread flour may be used instead. The high gluten content of the bread flour makes the dough easier to knead and roll out.

PASTA SHAPES

Each recipe in this book recommends the most suitable type of pasta for that particular sauce, but there are no strict rules and you can mix and match as you like. On the right are some of the varieties you can choose from.

Spaghetti
Long, thin, string-like strands.

Spaghettini
Thin spaghetti.

Tagliatelle
Long, flat, ribbon-like strands.

Tagliarini
Thin tagliatelle.

Fettucine
Long, thin, flat ribbons, slightly narrower than tagliatelle.

Linguine
Similar to spaghetti but slightly fatter.

Vermicelli
Long, thin strands.

Bucatini
Long, thin, hollow pasta.

Fusilli
Short, spiral-shaped.

Conchiglie
Shell-shaped.

Farfalle
Butterfly or bow-shaped.

Penne
Quill-shaped pasta tubes, ridged (*rigate*) or smooth.

Rigatoni
Short, fat, ridged tubes.

Ravioli
Filled squares of pasta.

Tortellini
Filled, curled semi-circles of pasta.

Pipe rigate
Curved, short, ridged tubes.

Lasagnette
Flat strips of pasta with wavy edges.

Fusilli bucati
Corkscrew twists.

Macaroni
Short, hollow tubes.

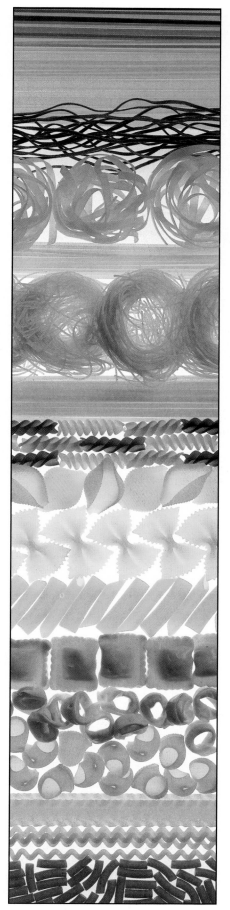

STORING PASTA

Dried pasta should be stored in a dry, dark place, where it will keep for up to 2 years. Fresh pasta has a much shorter shelf life and must be kept in the refrigerator, for no longer than 3 days. Fresh pasta can be frozen for up to 3 months. Layered or filled pasta, such as lasagne or ravioli, also freezes well, but cooked pasta in a sauce tends to become too soft when thawed.

COOKING PASTA

Pasta should always be cooked in a large pot containing plenty of fast-boiling water: 2 or 3 quarts per 1 lb. of pasta. You can add 1 or 2 teaspoons of salt or lemon juice to the cooking water for extra flavor. A teaspoon of oil added to the pot when the water is boiling will prevent the pasta from sticking together.

Once the water has reached a fast boil, add the pasta, stirring to separate it. Return the water to a boil, calculating the cooking time from the moment a rolling boil is reached. Leave the pot uncovered and stir the pasta occasionally.

Cooking times vary according to the type of pasta so it is always best to follow the guidelines on the package. As a guide, dried unfilled pasta takes 8 to 12 minutes, and dried filled pasta 15 to 20 minutes. Fresh unfilled pasta cooks in 2 or 3 minutes and fresh filled pasta in 7 to 10 minutes. Cooked pasta should be *al dente*, literally 'to the tooth', which means the pasta should be firm to the bite. As soon as the pasta is cooked, remove from the heat and drain in a colander or strainer. Do not rinse it.

Frozen fresh pasta does not need to be thawed before cooking.

QUANTITIES OF PASTA

In Italy, pasta is traditionally served as a first course, but most of the recipes in this book are intended to be served as a main course. For a main course, allow 3 or 4 oz. of dried pasta per person, or 4 or 5 oz. of fresh.

NUTRITIONAL CONTENT

The pasta given in the serving suggestions in this book is not included in the calorie counts and fat figures at the end of each recipe.

When cooked, 1 oz. of dried pasta contains:
94 Cals
0.6 g fat

BEEF & OYSTER

1/3 cup red wine
2 tablespoons dark soy sauce
2 tablespoons oyster sauce
2 garlic cloves, crushed
1 lb. lean beef round steak, cut into thin strips
2 teaspoons sunflower oil
1-inch piece fresh ginger root, peeled and finely
    chopped
1 bunch green onions, cut into 1/2-inch lengths
1 red bell pepper, sliced
3 carrots, cut into matchstick strips
1 tablespoon cornstarch
2/3 cup beef stock
Salt and freshly ground pepper
Flat-leaf parsley, to garnish

In a bowl, mix together red wine, soy sauce, oyster sauce and garlic. Add steak and stir until meat is coated with marinade. Cover, chill and marinate 1 hour. In a large skillet or wok, heat oil. Remove meat from marinade with a slotted spoon, reserving marinade, and add meat to pan with the ginger, green onions, bell pepper and carrots. Stir-fry meat and vegetables over high heat 3 to 5 minutes, until meat is browned and cooked through.

In a bowl, blend cornstarch with stock and marinade and add to the pan with salt and pepper. Bring to a boil over high heat, stirring continuously 1 or 2 minutes, until the sauce is thickened and glossy. Garnish with flat-leaf parsley and serve immediately with freshly cooked spaghetti.

Makes 4-3/4 cups or 6 servings.

Total Cals: 983	Total fat: 33.0 g
Cals per portion: 164	Fat per portion: 5.5 g
Cals per cup: 207	Fat per cup: 6.9 g

SMOKED HAM & LEEK

2 tablespoons low-fat margarine
1 lb. leeks, sliced
1/4 cup all-purpose flour
1-1/4 cups low-fat milk
1/4 cup chicken or vegetable stock
8 oz. cooked lean smoked ham, diced
1 teaspoon dried sage
Salt and freshly ground pepper
2 tablespoons half-and-half
Fresh sage, to garnish

In a saucepan, melt margarine over low heat. Add leeks and cook over low heat 8 minutes, stirring occasionally.

Stir in flour and cook 1 minute, stirring. Remove pan from heat and gradually stir in milk and stock. Bring slowly to a boil, stirring, and cook, stirring, until mixture thickens.

Add ham, sage, salt and pepper and simmer 5 minutes, stirring. Remove pan from heat and stir in half-and-half. Garnish with sage and serve with freshly cooked fettucine.

Makes 3-3/4 cups or 4 servings.

Total Cals: 738   Total fat: 32.5 g
Cals per portion: 185   Fat per portion: 8.1 g
Cals per cup: 197   Fat per cup: 8.7 g

Variation: Use smoked chicken in place of the smoked ham.

GROUND BEEF CHILE

1 teaspoon olive oil
1 large onion, chopped
1 red bell pepper, diced
1 garlic clove, crushed
1 lb. extra-lean ground beef
1 (8-oz.) can crushed tomatoes
1 (15-oz.) can red kidney beans, rinsed and drained
2/3 cup beef stock
2 tablespoons tomato paste
3 tablespoons dry sherry
2 teaspoons hot chile powder
1 teaspoon dried mixed herbs
1/2 teaspoon ground cumin
Salt and freshly ground pepper
Parsley sprigs, to garnish

In a large pan, heat oil and cook onion, red bell pepper and garlic 3 minutes. Add ground beef and cook, stirring, until browned all over.

Stir in tomatoes, kidney beans, stock, tomato paste, sherry, chile powder, herbs, cumin, salt and pepper and mix well. Bring slowly to a boil, reduce heat, cover and simmer 45 to 60 minutes, stirring occasionally. Garnish with parsley sprigs and serve with freshly cooked rigatoni.

Makes 4-1/2 cups or 6 servings.

Total Cals: 1192
Cals per portion: 199
Cals per cup: 265

Total fat: 45.7 g
Fat per portion: 7.6 g
Fat per cup: 10.1 g

—— PEPPERONI & FRESH CHILE ——

1 teaspoon sunflower oil
10 oz. leeks, thinly sliced
1 red bell pepper, sliced
1 fresh red chile, seeded and sliced
1 fresh green chile, seeded and sliced
1 garlic clove, crushed
1-1/4 lbs. tomatoes, peeled, seeded and chopped
3 oz. pepperoni, thinly sliced
1/2 teaspoon ground coriander
Salt and freshly ground pepper
Flat-leaf parsley, to garnish

In a large pan, heat oil. Add leeks, bell pepper, red and green chiles and garlic and cook 5 minutes.

Add tomatoes, pepperoni, coriander, salt and pepper, mixing well.

Bring slowly to a boil, reduce heat, cover and simmer 20 to 25 minutes, stirring occasionally. Garnish with parsley and serve with freshly cooked fusilli.

Makes 4 cups or 6 servings.

Total Cals: 688
Cals per portion: 115
Cals per cup: 172

Total fat: 47.5 g
Fat per portion: 7.9 g
Fat per cup: 11.9 g

Note: In place of fresh chiles, use chopped chile, available in jars.

—— PROSCIUTTO & TOMATO——

1 tablespoon low-fat margarine
4 shallots, finely chopped
1 tablespoon all-purpose flour
1-1/4 cups chicken or vegetable stock
1 (14-oz.) can crushed tomatoes
1 (8-oz.) can crushed tomatoes
1 tablespoon chopped fresh thyme
Dash of Worcestershire sauce
Salt and freshly ground pepper
4 oz. Prosciutto, cut into thin strips
Bay leaves and fresh thyme, to garnish

In a saucepan, melt margarine over low heat. Add shallots and cook 5 minutes, stirring occasionally.

Add flour and cook 1 minute, stirring. Remove pan from heat and gradually stir in stock. Bring slowly to a boil, stirring, and continue to cook, stirring, until the mixture thickens. Add tomatoes, thyme, Worcestershire sauce, salt and pepper and mix well. Return the mixture to a boil, reduce heat, cover and simmer 15 minutes, stirring occasionally.

Uncover and simmer 10 minutes to allow the sauce to thicken, stirring occasionally. Add Prosciutto and cook 3 minutes. Garnish with bay leaves and thyme and serve with freshly cooked filled pasta such as tortellini or ravioli.

Makes 3-1/4 cups or 4 servings.

Total Cals: 646	Total fat: 39.7 g
Cals per portion: 162	Fat per portion: 9.9 g
Cals per cup: 199	Fat per cup: 12.2 g

CHINESE-STYLE PORK

1/4 cup unsweetened apple juice
1/4 cup light soy sauce
2 tablespoons light brown sugar
1 tablespoon Worcestershire sauce
1 tablespoon tomato paste
2 teaspoons mustard powder
1 garlic clove, crushed
1 lb. lean pork fillet, cut into thin strips
1 teaspoon sunflower oil
1 bunch green onions, cut into 1/2-inch lengths
6 oz. small broccoli flowerets
6 oz. button mushrooms, halved
1 tablespoon cornstarch
Salt and freshly ground pepper
Shredded green onions, to garnish

In a bowl, mix together apple juice, soy sauce, sugar, Worcestershire sauce, tomato paste, mustard and garlic. Add pork and stir until the meat is covered with the marinade. Cover, and refrigerate 1 hour. In a large skillet or wok, heat oil. Remove pork from marinade with a slotted spoon, reserving marinade, and add pork to pan with green onions, broccoli and mushrooms. Stir-fry over high heat 5 to 7 minutes, until the meat is browned and cooked. Blend cornstarch with the marinade and 2 tablespoons water.

Add cornstarch mixture to the pan with salt and pepper. Bring to a boil over high heat, stirring continuously 1 or 2 minutes, until the sauce is thickened and glossy. Garnish with green onions and serve immediately with freshly cooked penne.

Makes 4 cups or 6 servings.

Total Cals: 1113
Cals per portion: 186
Cals per cup: 278

Total fat: 43.1 g
Fat per portion: 7.2 g
Fat per cup: 10.8 g

THAI-STYLE BEEF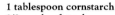

1 tablespoon cornstarch
2/3 cup beef stock
1/3 cup red wine
1 tablespoon dark soy sauce
Finely grated zest and juice of 1 lime
1 teaspoon each ground coriander and cumin
Salt and freshly ground pepper
2 teaspoons sesame oil
1 large onion, sliced
1 red bell pepper, sliced
1 fresh green chile, seeded and finely chopped
1-inch piece fresh ginger root, peeled and finely
    chopped
2 garlic cloves, crushed
1 lb. lean beef fillet, cut into thin strips
1 tablespoon sesame seeds

In a bowl, mix together cornstarch, stock, wine, soy sauce, lime zest and juice, coriander, cumin, salt and pepper and set aside. In a large skillet or wok, heat oil and stir-fry onion, bell pepper, chile, ginger and garlic 1 minute. Add beef and stir-fry 3 to 5 minutes, until the meat is browned and cooked through.

Add the cornstarch mixture and bring to a boil over high heat, stirring continuously 1 or 2 minutes, until the sauce is thickened and glossy. Sprinkle with sesame seeds, garnish with lemon wedges and cilantro leaves and serve immediately with freshly cooked tagliatelle.

Makes 3-1/4 cups or 4 servings.

Total Cals: 998   Total fat: 42.6 g
Cals per portion: 250   Fat per portion: 10.6 g
Cals per cup: 307   Fat per cup: 13.1 g

HAM & PINEAPPLE

1 (8-oz.) can pineapple chunks in fruit juice
4 oz. sugar snap peas
6 oz. low-fat cream cheese
2/3 cup low-fat plain yogurt
Salt and freshly ground pepper
12 oz. cooked lean ham steak, chopped
4 stalks celery, thinly sliced
2 tablespoons chopped fresh parsley
Chervil sprigs, to garnish

Drain pineapple, reserving 3 tablespoons of the juice. Finely chop half of the pineapple chunks, halve the remainder and set aside.

Cook sugar snap peas in boiling water 30 seconds. Drain, rinse in cold water and drain again. Set aside. Place the pineapple juice, cream cheese, yogurt, salt and pepper in a blender or food processor and blend until smooth.

Place in a bowl and stir in the ham, pineapple, celery, sugar snap peas and parsley and mix well. Garnish with chervil and serve with freshly cooked conchiglie.

Makes 5 cups or 4 servings.

Total Cals: 1051
Cals per portion: 263
Cals per cup: 210

Total fat: 31.9 g
Fat per portion: 8.0 g
Fat per cup: 6.4 g

BOLOGNESE

1 onion, chopped
1 garlic clove, crushed
1 lb. extra-lean ground beef
3 carrots, finely chopped
6 oz. mushrooms, sliced
3 stalks celery, sliced
1 (14-oz.) can crushed tomatoes
1 tablespoon tomato paste
2 teaspoons dried mixed herbs
1-1/4 cups beef stock
2/3 cup dry white wine
Salt and freshly ground pepper
Basil sprigs, to garnish

Place onion and garlic in a large saucepan with ground beef. Cook over low heat, stirring occasionally, until the ground beef is browned all over. Add carrots, mushrooms and celery to the pan and cook 5 minutes. Stir in tomatoes, tomato paste, mixed herbs, stock, wine, salt and pepper, mixing well. Bring slowly to a boil, cover and simmer 1 hour, stirring occasionally.

Uncover, increase heat slightly and simmer 30 minutes, to thicken the sauce. Garnish with basil sprigs and serve with freshly cooked spaghetti.

Makes 5-1/2 cups or 6 servings.

Total Cals: 1046   Total fat: 38.4 g
Cals per portion: 174   Fat per portion: 6.4 g
Cals per cup: 190   Fat per cup: 6.9 g

Variation: Use lean ground turkey or pork in place of the ground beef.

LIGHT CARBONARA

1 teaspoon olive oil
1 small onion, finely chopped
1 garlic clove, crushed
4 oz. cooked lean ham, cut into strips
3 eggs
1/2 cup grated Parmesan cheese
1/4 cup half-and-half
Salt and freshly ground pepper
Parsley leaves, to garnish

In a saucepan, heat oil and add onion and garlic. Cook over low heat 5 minutes. Add ham and mix well.

In a bowl, mix together eggs, grated Parmesan, half-and-half, salt and pepper. Remove saucepan from heat and stir in egg mixture.

Heat mixture very gently, stirring continuously, until the eggs just begin to set. Serve immediately, mixed into freshly cooked tagliatelle or spaghetti and garnished with parsley leaves.

Makes 2-1/4 cups or 6 servings.

Total Cals: 876   Total fat: 59.1 g
Cals per portion: 146   Fat per portion: 9.8 g
Cals per cup: 389   Fat per cup: 26.3 g

BEEF & MUSTARD

4 shallots, sliced
1 garlic clove, crushed
2/3 cup unsweetened red grape juice
1/4 cup red wine vinegar
1 tablespoon lemon juice
2 tablespoons whole grain mustard
1 tablespoon chopped fresh oregano
Salt and freshly ground pepper
1 lb. lean beef round steak, cubed
2 teaspoons sunflower oil
2 tablespoons all-purpose flour
2/3 cup beef stock
Fresh oregano, to garnish

In a bowl, mix together shallots, garlic, grape juice, vinegar, lemon juice, mustard, oregano, salt and pepper and mix well. Add steak and stir until meat is coated with marinade. Cover, and refrigerate 2 or 3 hours, stirring occasionally. In a large skillet or wok, heat oil. Remove steak and shallots from marinade with a slotted spoon, reserving marinade, and add steak and shallots to pan. Cook 5 minutes, stirring, until the meat is browned. Add the flour and cook 1 minute, stirring.

Remove pan from heat and gradually stir in stock and marinade. Bring slowly to a boil, stirring, and continue to cook until the mixture thickens. Simmer 8 to 10 minutes, until meat is tender, stirring occasionally. Garnish with oregano and serve with freshly cooked fusilli.

Makes 3-1/4 cups or 4 servings.

Total Cals: 903
Cals per portion: 226
Cals per cup: 278

Total fat: 35.0 g
Fat per portion: 8.8 g
Fat per cup: 10.7 g

SPICY PORK MEATBALLS

1 lb. lean ground pork
1 onion, finely chopped
1 garlic clove, crushed
1/2 cup fresh whole-wheat breadcrumbs
2 tablespoons tomato paste
1 egg, beaten
1 teaspoon ground coriander
1/2 teaspoon each ground bay leaves, allspice and
    cayenne pepper
4 teaspoons seasoned all-purpose flour
2 teaspoons olive oil
2 shallots, sliced
1 green and 1 red bell pepper, chopped
1 (14-oz.) can crushed tomatoes
2 teaspoons dried mixed herbs
2 teaspoons Worcestershire sauce

In a bowl, mix together pork, onion, garlic, breadcrumbs, 1 tablespoon tomato paste, egg and spices until thoroughly combined. Form the mixture into walnut-size balls and roll each ball in flour. Cover and chill 1 hour. In a skillet, heat 1 teaspoon of the oil and brown the meatballs all over, turning them carefully. In a large saucepan, heat remaining oil and cook shallots and bell peppers 5 minutes.

Add remaining 1 tablespoon tomato paste, tomatoes, mixed herbs and Worcestershire sauce and mix well. Bring to a boil. Add meatballs, stirring gently to cover them in sauce. Cover and simmer 20 minutes, stirring occasionally. Serve with freshly cooked linguine.

Makes 4-1/2 cups or 6 servings.

Total Cals: 1220
Cals per portion: 203
Cals per cup: 271

Total fat: 54.1 g
Fat per portion: 9.0 g
Fat per cup: 12.0 g

BEEF IN RED WINE

2 tablespoons all-purpose flour
Salt and freshly ground pepper
1 lb. lean beef chuck, cubed
2 tablespoons low-fat margarine
1 onion, chopped
2 oz. lean bacon, diced
2 carrots, sliced
4 oz. button mushrooms, halved
3/4 cup beef stock
3/4 cup red wine
2 teaspoons dried mixed herbs
Flat-leaf parsley and bay leaves, to garnish

Season flour with salt and pepper. Toss the beef in flour.

In a saucepan, melt margarine over low heat. Add beef, onion and bacon and cook 8 to 10 minutes, until the meat is browned all over. Add carrots to pan with mushrooms, stock, wine, mixed herbs, salt and pepper, mixing well.

Bring slowly to a boil, reduce heat, cover and simmer 1-1/2 to 2 hours, stirring occasionally. Garnish with flat-leaf parsley and bay leaves and serve with freshly cooked penne.

Makes 4-3/4 cups or 6 servings.

Total Cals: 1227
Cals per portion: 205
Cals per cup: 258

Total fat: 54.4 g
Fat per portion: 9.0 g
Fat per cup: 11.4 g

—HAM, MUSHROOM & PEPPER—

2 teaspoons sunflower oil
1 small green bell pepper, sliced
1 small red bell pepper, sliced
1 garlic clove, crushed
10 oz. mushrooms, sliced
1-1/4 cups chicken or vegetable stock
8 oz. cooked lean ham, finely diced
2 teaspoons Dijon mustard
Salt and freshly ground pepper
1 tablespoon cornstarch
3 tablespoons brandy
1 or 2 tablespoons chopped fresh basil
Basil sprigs, to garnish

In a large skillet or wok, heat oil and cook bell peppers and garlic 5 minutes. Add mushrooms and stock, cover and cook 5 minutes, stirring occasionally. Stir in ham, mustard, salt and pepper and cook 3 minutes. In a bowl, blend the cornstarch with brandy and add to pan.

Cook, stirring constantly, until mixture has thickened, then simmer 3 minutes. Stir in basil. Garnish with basil sprigs and serve with freshly cooked farfalle.

Makes 4 cups or 4 servings.

Total Cals: 622
Cals per portion: 155
Cals per cup: 155

Total fat: 24.7 g
Fat per portion: 6.1g
Fat per cup: 6.1 g

PEPPERED BEEF

1 lb. lean beef fillet, cut into thin strips
1 garlic clove, crushed
1 tablespoon black peppercorns, crushed
3 teaspoons olive oil
1 tablespoon cornstarch
2/3 cup beef stock
1/4 cup dry white wine
2 tablespoons dark soy sauce
Salt and freshly ground pepper
1 red bell pepper, sliced
1 bunch green onions, cut into 1/2-inch lengths
2 zucchini, cut into matchstick strips
Fresh cilantro, to garnish

In a bowl, mix together beef, garlic, peppercorns and 2 teaspoons oil. Cover and chill 3 or 4 hours, stirring occasionally. In another bowl, blend cornstarch with stock, wine, soy sauce, salt and pepper and set aside. In a large skillet or wok, heat the remaining 1 teaspoon oil and cook bell pepper, green onions and zucchini over high heat 3 minutes, stirring. Add beef mixture and cook 3 minutes, stirring, until meat is cooked through.

Add cornstarch mixture to the pan and cook, stirring continuously, until mixture thickens. Simmer 3 minutes. Garnish with cilantro and serve with freshly cooked rigatoni.

Makes 4 cups or 6 servings.

Total Cals: 942
Cals per portion: 157
Cals per cup: 236

Total fat: 38.4 g
Fat per portion: 6.4 g
Fat per cup: 9.6 g

CREAMED CELERY & HAM

1 small onion, sliced
1 small carrot, sliced
1 bay leaf
6 black peppercorns
1-1/4 cups low-fat milk
2 tablespoons low-fat margarine
1 onion, finely chopped
4 stalks celery, finely chopped
1/4 cup all-purpose flour
8 oz. cooked lean ham, finely chopped
1 tablespoon chopped fresh thyme
Salt and freshly ground pepper
2 tablespoons half-and-half
Fresh thyme, to garnish

Place onion, carrot, bay leaf and peppercorns in a saucepan with the milk and bring slowly to a boil. Remove pan from heat, cover and set aside 20 minutes. Strain milk into a bowl and discard the vegetables. In a saucepan, melt margarine over low heat. Add the chopped onion and celery, cover and cook 10 minutes, stirring occasionally. Stir in flour and cook 1 minute, stirring. Remove pan from heat and gradually stir in flavored milk.

Bring slowly to a boil, stirring, and continue to cook, stirring, until mixture thickens. Add ham, thyme, salt and pepper and simmer 5 minutes. Remove pan from heat and stir in half-and-half. Garnish with thyme and serve with freshly cooked filled pasta such as ravioli.

Makes 3-1/2 cups or 4 servings.

Total Cals: 711
Cals per portion: 178
Cals per cup: 203

Total fat: 30.8 g
Fat per portion: 7.7 g
Fat per cup: 8.8 g

MEXICAN PORK

2 tablespoons all-purpose flour
Salt and freshly ground pepper
1 lb. lean pork fillet, cubed
2 tablespoons low-fat margarine
2 onions, sliced
2 garlic cloves, crushed
1-1/4 cups tomato juice
1 (14-oz.) can crushed tomatoes
1 (15-oz.) can red kidney beans, rinsed and drained
1 teaspoon ground cumin
1/2 teaspoon ground coriander
1/2 teaspoon hot chile powder
1/2 teaspoon each dried basil and oregano
3 zucchini, sliced
Basil sprigs, to garnish

Season flour with salt and pepper. Toss pork fillet in flour. In a large saucepan, melt margarine over low heat. Add onions and garlic and cook 3 minutes. Add the pork and cook over low heat 3 to 5 minutes, stirring occasionally, until the meat is browned all over. Stir in tomato juice, tomatoes, kidney beans, spices, herbs, salt and pepper and mix well. Bring slowly to a boil, reduce heat, cover and simmer 1 to 1-1/2 hours, until the meat is tender, stirring occasionally.

Add zucchini 10 minutes before the end of cooking time. Garnish with basil sprigs and serve with freshly cooked tagliatelle or tagliarini.

Makes 5-3/4 cups or 6 servings.

Total Cals: 1404   Total fat: 49.4 g
Cals per portion: 234   Fat per portion: 8.2 g
Cals per cup: 244   Fat per cup: 8.6 g

Note: For authentic flavors and aromas, use a mortar and pestle to crush your own spices.

—— SHREDDED BEEF & GINGER ——

1 tablespoon cornstarch
3/4 cup beef stock
1/3 cup dry sherry
2 teaspoons sugar
Salt and freshly ground pepper
2 teaspoons olive oil
2 carrots, cut into matchstick strips
2-inch piece fresh ginger root, peeled and finely
    chopped
2 garlic cloves, crushed
12 oz. lean beef round steak, cut into thin strips
6 oz. snow peas

In a bowl, blend cornstarch with stock, sherry, sugar, salt and pepper and set aside. In a large skillet or wok, heat oil over high heat and stir-fry carrots, ginger and garlic 2 minutes. Add steak and stir-fry 3 minutes, until the meat is browned all over and cooked through. Add snow peas and stir-fry 1 minute.

Add cornstarch mixture and bring to a boil over high heat, stirring continuously 1 or 2 minutes, until sauce is thickened and glossy. Serve immediately with freshly cooked fusilli.

Makes 3-1/2 cups or 4 servings.

Total Cals: 850
Cals per portion: 213
Cals per cup: 243

Total fat: 27.3 g
Fat per portion: 6.8 g
Fat per cup: 7.8 g

— SPICY SAUSAGE & TOMATO —

1 lb. low-fat pork sausages
1 teaspoon sunflower oil
1 onion, sliced
1 garlic clove, crushed
1 fresh green chile, seeded and finely chopped
2 teaspoons dried thyme
2 teaspoons garam masala
1 teaspoon turmeric
1/2 teaspoon chile powder
6 oz. mushrooms, sliced
2/3 cup chicken or vegetable stock
1 (14-oz.) can crushed tomatoes
Salt and freshly ground pepper
Fresh thyme and parsley, to garnish

Add sausages to a skillet and cook 8 to 10 minutes or until browned all over. Cut into 1-inch pieces. In a saucepan, heat oil and cook onion, garlic and chile 5 minutes. Add thyme and spices and cook, stirring, 1 minute.

Add sausages, mushrooms, stock, tomatoes, salt and pepper. Mix gently but thoroughly and bring the mixture to a boil. Cover and simmer 20 minutes, stirring occasionally, until the sausages are cooked through. Garnish with thyme and parsley and serve with freshly cooked penne.

Makes 5-1/4 cups or 6 servings.

Total Cals: 1026   Total fat: 52.9 g
Cals per portion: 171   Fat per portion: 8.8 g
Cals per cup: 195   Fat per cup: 10.0 g

BEEF & SNOW PEA

1 tablespoon cornstarch
2/3 cup beef stock
1/3 cup tomato juice
1 tablespoon tomato paste
2 tablespoons dark soy sauce
2 teaspoons Worcestershire sauce
1 tablespoon light brown sugar
Salt and freshly ground pepper
2 teaspoons walnut oil
2 garlic cloves, crushed
1 bunch green onions, cut into 1/2-inch lengths
4 stalks celery, thinly sliced
2-inch piece fresh ginger root, peeled and finely
    chopped
1 (1-lb.) lean beef round steak, cubed
8 oz. snow peas

In a bowl, blend cornstarch with stock, tomato juice, tomato paste, soy sauce, Worcestershire sauce, sugar, salt and pepper. Set aside. In a large skillet or wok, heat oil and add garlic, green onions, celery and ginger and stir-fry over high heat 1 minute. Add beef and stir-fry 3 to 5 minutes, until meat is browned. Add snow peas and cook 1 minute.

Add cornstarch mixture to pan and bring to a boil over high heat, stirring continuously 1 or 2 minutes, until the sauce is thickened and glossy. Serve immediately with freshly cooked fettucine or tagliatelle.

Makes 4-1/2 cups or 6 servings.

Total Cals: 934
Cals per portion: 156
Cals per cup: 208

Total fat: 32.8 g
Fat per portion: 5.5 g
Fat per cup: 7.3 g

——SMOKED HAM & TOMATO——

1-1/2 lbs. tomatoes, peeled, seeded and chopped
8 oz. leeks, sliced
2 carrots, finely diced
2 stalks celery, thinly sliced
1 garlic clove, crushed
1 tablespoon tomato paste
2 teaspoons sugar
Dash of Tabasco sauce
Salt and freshly ground pepper
6 oz. cooked lean smoked ham, diced
1 or 2 tablespoons chopped fresh basil
2 tablespoons half-and-half
Basil sprigs, to garnish

Place tomatoes, leeks, carrots, celery, garlic, tomato paste, sugar, Tabasco sauce, salt and pepper in a saucepan and mix well. Bring slowly to a boil, reduce heat, cover and simmer 10 minutes, stirring occasionally. Stir in ham and cook 10 minutes, stirring occasionally.

Remove pan from heat and stir in basil and half-and-half. Garnish with basil sprigs and serve with freshly cooked rigatoni or conchiglie.

Makes 4-1/2 cups or 4 servings.

Total Cals: 545   Total fat: 15.9 g
Cals per portion: 136   Fat per portion: 3.9 g
Cals per cup: 121   Fat per cup: 3.5 g

Note: If tomato mixture is too dry, add 1/4 cup water when you add the ham.

—PROSCIUTTO & ASPARAGUS—

12 oz. asparagus
2 teaspoons walnut oil
1 onion, finely chopped
1 garlic clove, crushed
4 oz. Prosciutto, cut into thin strips
1 tablespoon cornstarch
3/4 cup vegetable stock
1/3 cup dry white wine
1 tablespoon light soy sauce
2 teaspoons Dijon mustard
Salt and freshly ground pepper
Rosemary sprigs, to garnish

Trim the woody ends from the asparagus and cut the spears into 1/2-inch lengths.

In a saucepan, heat oil over high heat and cook asparagus, onion and garlic 5 minutes. Reduce heat, add Prosciutto and cook 1 minute. In a bowl, blend cornstarch, stock, wine, soy sauce, mustard, salt and pepper and add to the pan.

Bring to a boil, stirring, and continue to cook, stirring, until mixture thickens. Simmer 5 minutes. Garnish with rosemary sprigs and serve with freshly cooked linguine.

Makes 2-1/2 cups or 3 servings.

Total Cals: 721
Cals per portion: 240
Cals per cup: 288

Total fat: 45.4 g
Fat per portion: 15.1 g
Fat per cup: 18.1 g

─COUNTRY-STYLE CHICKEN─

2 teaspoons olive oil
1 onion, sliced
2 garlic cloves, crushed
1 green bell pepper, sliced
2 carrots, sliced
1 lb. skinless, boneless chicken breasts, cut into thin
    strips
2 oz. lean bacon, diced
6 oz. button mushrooms
2 cups chicken stock
3 tablespoons tomato paste
1 teaspoon dried mixed herbs
Salt and freshly ground pepper
1 tablespoon cornstarch
Marjoram sprigs, to garnish

In a large skillet or wok, heat oil, add onion, garlic, bell pepper and carrots and cook 5 minutes. Add the chicken and bacon and cook until the chicken is lightly browned all over, stirring occasionally. Stir in mushrooms, stock, tomato paste, mixed herbs, salt and pepper, mixing well. Bring slowly to a boil, reduce heat, cover and simmer 15 minutes, until chicken is cooked and tender, stirring occasionally.

In a small bowl, blend cornstarch with 2 tablespoons water and add to pan. Bring back to a boil and continue to cook, stirring continuously, until the mixture thickens. Simmer 2 or 3 minutes. Garnish with marjoram sprigs and serve with freshly cooked tagliatelle.

Makes 5-3/4 cups or 6 servings

Total Cals: 1040	Total fat: 48.4 g
Cals per portion: 173	Fat per portion: 8.0 g
Cals per cup: 181	Fat per cup: 8.4 g

──CHICKEN IN WHITE WINE──

2 tablespoons low-fat margarine
1 shallot, thinly sliced
8 oz. mushrooms, sliced
1/4 cup all-purpose flour
1/2 cup chicken stock
3/4 cup dry white wine
1 lb. cooked chicken, cubed
4 oz. seedless grapes, halved
Salt and freshly ground pepper
2 tablespoons half-and-half
1 tablespoon chopped fresh tarragon
Tarragon sprigs, to garnish

In a saucepan, melt margarine and cook shallot and mushrooms 5 minutes.

Add flour and cook 1 minute, stirring. Gradually stir in stock and wine. Bring slowly to a boil, stirring, and continue to cook until mixture thickens.

Add the chicken to sauce with the grapes, salt and pepper and simmer 5 minutes, stirring. Remove pan from heat and stir in half-and-half and tarragon. Garnish with tarragon sprigs and serve with freshly cooked spaghettini or tagliarini.

Makes 4-1/4 cups or 6 servings.

Total Cals: 1168
Cals per portion: 195
Cals per cup: 275

Total fat: 36.7 g
Fat per portion: 6.1 g
Fat per cup: 8.6 g

CHICKEN ITALIENNE

2 tablespoons all-purpose flour
Salt and freshly ground pepper
1 lb. skinless, boneless chicken breasts, cubed
2 teaspoons olive oil
12 oz. pearl onions, halved
1 garlic clove, crushed
1 cup chicken stock
3/4 cup dry white wine
1 (8-oz.) can crushed tomatoes
1 tablespoon tomato paste
1 tablespoon chopped fresh mixed herbs
Flat-leaf parsley, to garnish

Season flour with salt and pepper. Toss chicken in flour.

In a large saucepan, heat oil and cook onions and garlic 5 minutes. Add chicken and cook until lightly browned all over. Gradually stir in stock and wine, then add tomatoes, tomato paste, herbs, salt and pepper, mixing well.

Bring slowly to a boil, reduce heat, cover and simmer 25 minutes, stirring occasionally, until the chicken is cooked and tender. Garnish with parsley and serve with freshly cooked linguine or fettucine.

Makes 5-1/4 cups or 6 servings.

Total Cals: 1026
Cals per portion: 171
Cals per cup: 195

Total fat: 25.7 g
Fat per portion: 4.3 g
Fat per cup: 4.9 g

—PIQUANT CHICKEN & HAM—

3 tablespoons low-fat margarine
1/3 cup all-purpose flour
2 cups low-fat milk
2 teaspoons tandoori powder
1 teaspoon garam masala
8 oz. cooked chicken, diced
8 oz. cooked lean ham, cut into strips
Salt and freshly ground pepper
2 tablespoons chopped fresh parsley
Fresh cilantro, to garnish

In a large saucepan, melt margarine over low
heat. Add flour and cook 1 minute, stirring.

Remove pan from heat and gradually stir in
milk. Bring slowly to a boil, stirring, and
continue to cook, stirring, until mixture
thickens.

Add spices, chicken, ham, salt and pepper
and simmer 5 minutes, stirring. Stir in
parsley. Garnish with fresh cilantro and serve
with freshly cooked conchiglie.

Makes 3-1/2 cups or 6 servings.

Total Cals: 1212
Cals per portion: 202
Cals per cup: 346

Total fat: 50.5 g
Fat per portion: 8.4 g
Fat per cup: 14.4 g

‒MARINATED TURKEY & MINT‒

1/2 cup dry white wine
2 tablespoons light soy sauce
1 tablespoon lemon juice
1 garlic clove, crushed
1/4 cup chopped fresh mint
1 lb. skinless turkey scallops, cut into thin strips
2 teaspoons sunflower oil
1 onion, sliced
4 carrots, cut into matchstick strips
3 zucchini, thinly sliced
1 tablespoon cornstarch
1-1/4 cups chicken stock
Salt and freshly ground pepper
Mint sprigs, to garnish

In a bowl, mix together wine, soy sauce, lemon juice, garlic and 2 tablespoons mint. Add turkey and mix well. Cover and refrigerate 2 or 3 hours. In a large skillet or wok, heat oil over high heat and stir-fry onion, carrots and zucchini 2 minutes. Remove turkey from marinade with a slotted spoon, reserving marinade, and add turkey to pan. Stir-fry over high heat 3 or 4 minutes, until turkey is cooked.

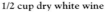

In a bowl, blend cornstarch with marinade and stock and add to pan with salt and pepper. Bring to a boil over high heat, stirring 1 or 2 minutes, until sauce is thickened and glossy. Add remaining mint. Garnish with mint sprigs and serve immediately with freshly cooked spaghetti.

Makes 5-1/2 cups or 6 servings.

Total Cals: 964	Total fat: 18.3 g
Cals per portion: 161	Fat per portion: 3.0 g
Cals per cup: 175	Fat per cup: 3.3 g

CHICKEN & MUSHROOM

3 tablespoons low-fat margarine
2 leeks, thinly sliced
8 oz. mushrooms, sliced
1/3 cup all-purpose flour
1-1/4 cups low-fat milk
2/3 cup chicken stock
12 oz. cooked chicken, cut into small pieces
Salt and freshly ground pepper
1 tablespoon chopped fresh parsley
Parsley sprigs, to garnish

In a saucepan, melt margarine over low heat. Add leeks and mushrooms, cover and cook over low heat 8 minutes or until soft, stirring occasionally.

Add flour and cook 1 minute, stirring. Remove pan from heat and gradually stir in milk and stock. Bring slowly to a boil, stirring, and continue to cook, stirring, until the mixture thickens.

Add chicken, salt and pepper and simmer 5 minutes, stirring. Stir in the parsley. Garnish with parsley sprigs and serve with freshly cooked fusilli.

Makes 5-1/2 cups or 6 servings.

Total Cals: 1139
Cals per portion: 190
Cals per cup: 207

Total fat: 43.7 g
Fat per portion: 7.3 g
Fat per cup: 7.9 g

Variation: Use chopped fresh tarragon or cilantro in place of the parsley.

SWEET & SOUR CHICKEN

2 tablespoons each light soy sauce and dry sherry
1 lb. skinless, boneless chicken breasts, cut into thin
    strips
2 teaspoons walnut oil
1 red bell pepper, sliced
1 bunch green onions, cut into 1/2-inch lengths
3 carrots, thinly sliced
3 stalks celery, thinly sliced
1 garlic clove, crushed
2 tablespoons cornstarch
2/3 cup chicken stock
2/3 cup unsweetened apple juice
2 tablespoons white wine vinegar
2 tablespoons tomato paste
3 tablespoons honey
Green onion strips, to garnish

In a bowl, mix together soy sauce, sherry and chicken. Cover and leave to marinate 30 minutes. In a large skillet or wok, heat oil over high heat and stir-fry bell pepper, green onions, carrots, celery and garlic 3 minutes. Remove chicken from marinade using a slotted spoon, reserving marinade, and add chicken to pan. Stir-fry over high heat 5 minutes, until the chicken is cooked.

In a measuring jug, blend cornstarch with marinade, stock, apple juice, vinegar, tomato paste and honey and add to pan. Bring to a boil, stirring, until sauce has thickened. Simmer 3 minutes, stirring. Garnish with green onion strips and serve with freshly cooked tagliatelle or spaghetti.

Makes 5-1/2 cups or 6 servings.

Total Cals: 1144   Total fat: 27.5 g
Cals per portion: 191   Fat per portion: 4.6 g
Cals per cup: 208   Fat per cup: 5.0 g

CHICKEN & CORN

4 oz. frozen green peas or petits pois
1 cup low-fat plain fromage frais
1/4 cup regular plain yogurt
1/4 cup reduced-calorie mayonnaise
1 (8-oz.) can whole-kernel corn, drained
8 green onions, thinly sliced
12 oz. cooked chicken, cubed
1 tablespoon chopped fresh cilantro
Salt and freshly ground pepper
Chopped fresh chives, to garnish

In a pan of boiling water, cook peas 3 to 5 minutes or just until tender. Drain and cool. In a bowl, mix together fromage frais, yogurt and mayonnaise.

Add cooled peas, corn, green onions, chicken, cilantro, salt and pepper and mix gently but thoroughly. Garnish with chives and serve with freshly cooked farfalle.

Makes 4 cups or 6 servings.

Total Cals: 1300
Cals per portion: 217
Cals per cup: 325

Total fat: 44.9 g
Fat per portion: 7.5 g
Fat per cup: 11.2 g

Variation: Use other meats or fish such as ham, turkey or tuna, in place of the chicken.

— LEMON CHICKEN WITH BASIL —

Finely grated zest of 1 lemon
Juice of 2 lemons
2 garlic cloves, crushed
3 teaspoons olive oil
1/4 cup chopped fresh basil
Salt and freshly ground pepper
1 lb. skinless, boneless chicken breasts, cubed
1 onion, sliced
3 stalks celery, thinly sliced
6 oz. button mushrooms, halved
2 tablespoons all-purpose flour
2/3 cup chicken stock
2/3 cup dry white wine
Lemon zest, lemon twists and basil sprigs, to garnish

In a bowl, mix together lemon zest, lemon juice, garlic, 2 teaspoons of the oil, 2 tablespoons basil, salt and pepper. Add chicken and mix well. Cover and chill 1 hour. Heat remaining 1 teaspoon oil in a large skillet or wok and cook onion 3 minutes. Remove chicken from marinade with a slotted spoon, reserving marinade, and add chicken to the pan. Cook until chicken is lightly browned. Add celery and mushrooms and cook 2 minutes.

Add flour and cook 1 minute, stirring. Remove pan from heat and gradually add stock, wine and marinade. Bring to a boil and cook, stirring, until the mixture thickens. Cover and simmer 15 minutes, stirring occasionally. Stir in remaining basil. Garnish and serve with freshly cooked linguine.

Makes 4 cups or 4 servings.

Total Cals: 972   Total fat: 31.5 g
Cals per portion: 243   Fat per portion: 7.9 g
Cals per cup: 243   Fat per cup: 7.9 g

CHICKEN & MANGO

2 teaspoons olive oil
1 onion, chopped
2 garlic cloves, crushed
12 oz. skinless, boneless chicken breasts, cubed
3 tablespoons all-purpose flour
1-1/2 cups chicken stock
1 cup dry white wine
Salt and freshly ground pepper
1/3 cup raisins
1 ripe mango
2 tablespoons chopped fresh parsley

In a large saucepan, heat oil and cook onion and garlic 3 minutes.

Add chicken and cook until lightly browned all over. Sprinkle with flour and cook 1 minute, stirring. Remove pan from heat and gradually stir in stock and wine. Add salt and pepper and bring slowly to a boil, stirring continuously. Cover and simmer 30 minutes, stirring occasionally. Stir in raisins and cook another 10 minutes.

Peel and pit mango and puree flesh in a blender or food processor until smooth. Add mango puree and parsley to pan and cook over low heat 5 minutes, until the sauce is warmed through. Serve with freshly cooked penne.

Makes 4-1/2 cups or 6 servings.

Total Cals: 1152
Cals per portion: 192
Cals per cup: 256

Total fat: 22.7 g
Fat per portion: 3.4 g
Fat per cup: 5.0 g

—— CREAMY SPICED CHICKEN ——

2/3 cup tomato juice
1 onion, chopped
1 garlic clove, crushed
1-inch piece fresh ginger root, peeled and chopped
1 fresh green chile, seeded and chopped
Juice of 1 lemon
2 teaspoons olive oil
2 teaspoons paprika
1 teaspoon each garam masala and ground cumin
Salt and freshly ground pepper
1 lb. skinless, boneless chicken breasts, cubed
2/3 cup half-and-half
1 or 2 tablespoons chopped fresh cilantro
Fresh cilantro, to garnish

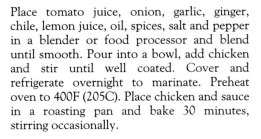

Place tomato juice, onion, garlic, ginger, chile, lemon juice, oil, spices, salt and pepper in a blender or food processor and blend until smooth. Pour into a bowl, add chicken and stir until well coated. Cover and refrigerate overnight to marinate. Preheat oven to 400F (205C). Place chicken and sauce in a roasting pan and bake 30 minutes, stirring occasionally.

Remove from oven and stir in half-and-half and cilantro. Return chicken to oven and cook another 10 minutes, until sauce has warmed through. Garnish with cilantro and serve with freshly cooked rigatoni.

Makes 3-1/2 cups or 6 servings.

Total Cals: 986	Total fat: 42.2 g
Cals per portion: 164	Fat per portion: 7.0 g
Cals per cup: 282	Fat per cup: 12.0 g

SMOKED TURKEY

3/4 cup low-fat plain yogurt
1/4 cup reduced-calorie mayonnaise
1/4 cup regular plain yogurt
8 oz. cooked, lean smoked turkey
6 oz. radishes
4 oz. sugar snap peas
2 tablespoons chopped fresh tarragon
Salt and freshly ground pepper
Tarragon sprigs, to garnish

In a bowl, mix together low-fat yogurt, mayonnaise and regular plain yogurt.

Cut turkey into thin strips. Remove tops and roots from radishes and ends from sugar snap peas and slice. Add to yogurt mixture with turkey and mix well.

Add chopped tarragon, salt and pepper and mix well. Garnish with tarragon sprigs and serve with freshly cooked tagliatelle or spaghettini.

Makes 3-3/4 cups or 4 servings.

Total Cals: 725   Total fat: 30.1 g
Cals per portion: 181   Fat per portion: 7.5 g
Cals per cup: 193   Fat per cup: 8.0 g

Variation: Use smoked chicken in place of the turkey and cilantro or mint in place of the tarragon.

CHICKEN A L'ORANGE

2 tablespoons low-fat margarine
1 lb. pearl onions, halved
1 lb. skinless, boneless chicken breasts, cubed
2 tablespoons all-purpose flour
8 oz. button mushrooms
Grated zest of 1 large orange
Juice of 3 large oranges
2/3 cup unsweetened apple juice
1 tablespoon light brown sugar
Salt and freshly ground pepper
2 tablespoons chopped fresh parsley
Orange slices and flat-leaf parsley, to garnish

In a large saucepan, melt margarine add onions and cook 5 minutes.

Add chicken and cook until lightly browned all over. Sprinkle with flour and cook 1 minute, stirring. Add mushrooms and orange zest, then gradually stir in orange juice, apple juice, sugar, salt and pepper, mixing well.

Bring slowly to a boil, stirring, then cover and simmer 20 minutes, stirring occasionally. Stir in parsley. Garnish with orange slices and flat-leaf parsley and serve with freshly cooked fusilli.

Makes 5-1/4 cups or 6 servings.

Total Cals: 1046	Total fat: 27.0 g
Cals per portion: 174	Fat per portion: 4.5 g
Cals per cup: 199	Fat per cup: 5.1 g

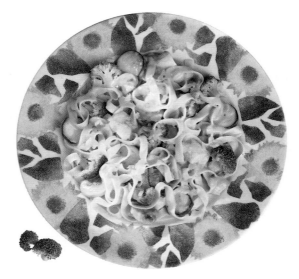

CHICKEN & BROCCOLI

6 oz. small broccoli flowerets
2 tablespoons low-fat margarine
1 small onion, finely chopped
2 zucchini, sliced
4 oz. mushrooms, sliced
1/4 cup all-purpose flour
2/3 cup low-fat milk
3/4 cup chicken stock
12 oz. cooked chicken, cubed
Salt and freshly ground pepper
1 tablespoon chopped fresh oregano

Steam broccoli over a pan of boiling water 4 or 5 minutes or until tender. Set aside.

In a saucepan, melt margarine over low heat. Add onion, zucchini and mushrooms, cover and cook 10 minutes, stirring occasionally. Stir in flour and cook 1 minute, stirring. Remove from heat and gradually stir in milk and stock. Bring slowly to a boil, stirring, and continue to cook, stirring, until mixture thickens.

Add broccoli, chicken, salt, pepper and oregano and simmer 5 minutes, stirring occasionally. Serve with freshly cooked tagliatelle or spaghetti.

Makes 4-3/4 cups or 6 servings.

Total Cals: 984	Total fat: 33.6 g
Cals per portion: 164	Fat per portion: 5.6 g
Cals per cup: 207	Fat per cup: 7.0 g

TURKEY & GINGER

2 teaspoons sunflower oil
1 onion, sliced
3 carrots, thinly sliced
2 stalks celery, thinly sliced
2 zucchini, thinly sliced
2-inch piece fresh ginger root, peeled and finely
    chopped
12 oz. skinless turkey breasts, cut into strips
1 tablespoon cornstarch
2/3 cup sweet sherry
1/2 cup chicken stock
1/4 cup unsweetened orange juice
Salt and freshly ground pepper
Flat-leaf parsley, to garnish

In a large skillet or wok, heat oil over high heat. Add onion, carrots, celery, zucchini, ginger and turkey and stir-fry 5 to 7 minutes, until the turkey is cooked through. In a small bowl, blend cornstarch with the sherry, stock and orange juice and add to pan with salt and pepper.

Bring to a boil and cook over high heat, stirring continuously, 1 or 2 minutes, until sauce is thickened and glossy. Garnish with flat-leaf parsley and serve with freshly cooked linguine.

Makes 4-3/4 cups or 6 servings.

Total Cals: 967   Total fat: 16.7 g
Cals per portion: 161   Fat per portion: 2.8 g
Cals per cup: 204   Fat per cup: 3.5 g

SPICY SHRIMP

2 teaspoons sunflower oil
1 bunch green onions, cut into 1/2-inch lengths
2 garlic cloves, crushed
1 small fresh red chile, seeded and finely chopped
6 oz. button mushrooms, halved
1 teaspoon ground coriander
1 teaspoon ground cumin
1 teaspoon ground turmeric
1/2 teaspoon ground ginger
2/3 cup fish or chicken stock
1/3 cup dry sherry
Salt and freshly ground pepper
1 lb. cooked, peeled large shrimp
1 tablespoon cornstarch
Fresh cilantro, to garnish

In a saucepan, heat oil and cook green onions, garlic and chile 2 minutes. Add mushrooms and spices and cook, stirring, 1 minute. Stir in stock, sherry, salt and pepper. Bring to a boil, reduce heat, cover and simmer 5 minutes, stirring occasionally. Add shrimp and cook 1 minute.

In a small bowl, blend cornstarch with 2 tablespoons water and add to pan. Bring back to a boil, stirring continuously, until mixture thickens. Simmer 3 minutes. Garnish with cilantro and serve with freshly cooked spaghetti or tagliarini.

Makes 3-3/4 cups or 4 servings.

Total Cals: 795
Cals per portion: 199
Cals per cup: 212

Total fat: 22.6 g
Fat per portion: 5.6 g
Fat per cup: 6.0 g

SALMON & ZUCCHINI

2 tablespoons low-fat margarine
2 zucchini, cut into matchstick strips
2 shallots, finely chopped
1/4 cup all-purpose flour
1-1/4 cups low-fat milk
1 (7-1/2-oz.) can salmon in water, drained and flaked
Dash of Tabasco sauce
1 tablespoon chopped fresh chives
Salt and freshly ground pepper
Lemon slices and chives, to garnish

In a saucepan, melt margarine over low heat. Add zucchini and shallots and cook 8 minutes, stirring occasionally.

Stir in flour and cook 1 minute, stirring. Remove pan from heat and gradually stir in milk. Bring slowly to a boil, stirring, and continue to cook, stirring, until mixture thickens.

Add salmon, Tabasco sauce, chives, salt and pepper and simmer 5 minutes, stirring. Garnish with lemon slices and chives and serve with freshly cooked conchiglie.

Makes 3-1/2 cups or 4 servings.

Total Cals: 743	Total fat: 35.9 g
Cals per portion: 186	Fat per portion: 8.9 g
Cals per cup: 212	Fat per cup: 10.3 g

Variation: Use tuna in place of the salmon.

SHRIMP & MUSHROOM

2 teaspoons sunflower oil
1 onion, chopped
1 green bell pepper, chopped
1 garlic clove, crushed
2 tablespoons fresh thyme leaves
8 oz. button mushrooms, halved
3 tomatoes, peeled, seeded and chopped
3/4 cup fish or chicken stock
1/2 cup dry white wine
Salt and freshly ground pepper
1 lb. cooked, peeled jumbo shrimp, thawed and
   drained if frozen
1 tablespoon cornstarch

In a saucepan, heat oil and cook onion, green bell pepper and garlic 5 minutes.

Chop half of the thyme reserving remainder for garnish. Add mushrooms, tomatoes, stock, wine, chopped thyme, salt and pepper and mix well. Bring to a boil, reduce heat, cover and simmer 10 minutes, stirring occasionally. Add shrimp and cook 5 minutes. In a bowl, blend cornstarch with 2 tablespoons water and add to pan.

Bring back to a boil, stirring continuously, until mixture has thickened. Simmer 3 minutes. Garnish with reserved thyme leaves and serve with freshly cooked linguine or fettucine.

Makes 5-1/4 cups or 6 servings.

Total Cals: 857
Cals per portion: 143
Cals per cup: 163

Total fat: 21.2 g
Fat per portion: 3.5 g
Fat per cup: 4.0 g

TUNA & ANCHOVY

2 teaspoons olive oil
3 shallots, finely chopped
1 garlic clove, crushed
8 oz. mushrooms, sliced
3/4 cup fish or chicken stock
2/3 cup dry white wine
1 (7-oz.) can tuna in water, drained and flaked
1 (3-1/2-oz.) can anchovies, rinsed, drained and
  chopped
1 tablespoon capers, chopped
Salt and freshly ground pepper
1 tablespoon cornstarch
1 tablespoon chopped fresh parsley
Fresh parsley, to garnish

In a saucepan, heat oil and cook shallots and garlic 1 minute. Add mushrooms, cover and cook 5 minutes, stirring occasionally. Stir in stock, wine, tuna, anchovies, capers, salt and pepper and mix well. Bring to a boil and simmer 3 minutes, stirring.

In a small bowl, blend cornstarch with 2 tablespoons water and add to pan. Bring back to a boil, stirring continuously, until the mixture has thickened. Simmer 3 minutes, then stir in chopped parsley just before serving. Garnish with parsley and serve with freshly cooked penne.

Makes 3-3/4 cups or 4 servings.

Total Cals: 798   Total fat: 32.7 g
Cals per portion: 199   Fat per portion: 8.1 g
Cals per cup: 213   Fat per cup: 8.7 g

— SMOKED TROUT WITH LIME —

10 oz. smoked trout fillets
1-1/4 cups low-fat plain fromage frais or yogurt
1/4 cup reduced-calorie mayonnaise
2 tablespoons horseradish
Grated zest and juice of 1 lime
2 tablespoons chopped fresh parsley
Salt and freshly ground pepper
5 oz. sugar snap peas, diagonally sliced
5 stalks celery, cut into matchstick strips
Lime slices and parsley sprigs, to garnish

Skin trout and discard any bones. Cut flesh
into small pieces and set aside.

In a large bowl, mix together fromage frais,
mayonnaise, horseradish, lime zest, lime
juice, parsley, salt and pepper, until
thoroughly combined.

Add trout, sugar snap peas and celery and
mix well. Garnish with lime slices and
parsley and serve with freshly cooked farfalle
or conchiglie.

Makes 4 cups or 6 servings.

Total Cals: 878   Total fat: 34.6 g
Cals per portion: 146   Fat per portion: 5.7 g
Cals per cup: 219   Fat per cup: 8.6 g

SPICED SEAFOOD

2/3 cup fish or chicken stock, cooled
2/3 cup dry white wine
2 tablespoons tomato paste
1-1/2 teaspoons each ground coriander and cumin
1 teaspoon each chile powder and ground ginger
1/2 teaspoon turmeric
1 lb. cooked mixed seafood
2 teaspoons olive oil
1 onion, chopped
1 garlic clove, crushed
1 red bell pepper, sliced
1 (8-oz.) can whole-kernel corn, drained
Salt and freshly ground pepper
1 tablespoon cornstarch
2 tablespoons chopped fresh cilantro
Cilantro sprigs, to garnish

In a bowl, mix together stock, wine, tomato paste and spices. Add seafood and mix well. Cover, and refrigerate 1 hour. In a saucepan, heat oil and add onion, garlic and bell pepper. Cover and cook over low heat 10 minutes, stirring occasionally. Add the seafood, marinade, corn, salt and pepper and mix well. Bring to a boil and simmer 5 minutes, stirring occasionally. In a bowl, blend cornstarch with 2 tablespoons water and add to pan.

Bring back to a boil, stirring continuously, until mixture thickens. Simmer 3 minutes. Stir in cilantro just before serving. Garnish with cilantro and serve with freshly cooked tagliatelle or spaghetti.

Makes 5-1/4 cups or 6 servings.

Total Cals: 1000   Total fat: 23.4 g
Cals per portion: 167   Fat per portion: 3.9 g
Cals per cup: 190   Fat per cup: 4.4 g

Note: Buy a pack of mixed seafood or use large shrimp and scallops.

COD IN WHITE WINE

3 tablespoons low-fat margarine
2 zucchini, diagonally sliced
3 shallots, thinly sliced
1/3 cup all-purpose flour
3/4 cup fish or chicken stock
3/4 cup dry white wine
2 tablespoons chopped fresh mixed herbs
Salt and freshly ground pepper
1 lb. cod fillet, skinned and cubed
Fresh parsley, to garnish

Preheat oven to 375F (190C). In a large saucepan, melt margarine over low heat. Add zucchini and shallots and cook 3 minutes.

Stir in flour and cook 1 minute, stirring. Remove pan from heat and gradually stir in stock and wine. Bring slowly to a boil, stirring, and cook, stirring, until the mixture thickens.

Add herbs, salt, pepper and fish and mix gently but thoroughly. Transfer to an ovenproof dish. Cover and cook in the oven 20 to 25 minutes, stirring once. Garnish with parsley and serve with freshly cooked spaghetti or linguine.

Makes 4-1/2 cups or 4 servings.

Total Cals: 870
Cals per portion: 218
Cals per cup: 193

Total fat: 23.5 g
Fat per portion: 5.9 g
Fat per cup: 5.2 g

TUNA & CHILE BEAN

3/4 cup low-fat plain fromage frais or yogurt
1/2 cup reduced-calorie mayonnaise
1 or 2 teaspoons chile powder
2 tablespoons chopped fresh mixed herbs
1 bunch green onions, cut into 1/2-inch lengths
3 stalks celery, thinly sliced
1 (14-oz.) can tuna in water, drained and flaked
1 (15-oz.) can red kidney beans, rinsed and drained
Salt and freshly ground pepper
Fresh parsley, to garnish

In a bowl, mix together fromage frais, mayonnaise, chile powder and herbs.

Add green onions, celery, tuna, red kidney beans, salt and pepper, mixing well. Chill until ready to serve. Garnish with parsley and serve with freshly cooked fusilli.

Makes 4-3/4 cups or 6 servings.

Total Cals: 1252   Total fat: 36.2 g
Cals per portion: 209   Fat per portion: 6.0 g
Cals per cup: 264   Fat per cup: 7.6 g

Variation: Use canned salmon or sardines in place of the tuna.

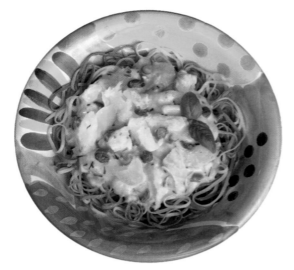

— SMOKED HADDOCK & CAPER —

2 cups low-fat milk
1 bay leaf
1 lb. smoked haddock fillets, skinned
2 tablespoons low-fat margarine
1 onion, finely chopped
1/4 cup all-purpose flour
2 tablespoons capers, halved
1 tablespoon chopped fresh chives
Salt and freshly ground pepper
Basil sprigs, to garnish

Pour milk into a large skillet, add bay leaf and smoked haddock and bring slowly to a boil. Cover and simmer 15 to 20 minutes, until fish is cooked.

Strain milk into a bowl and set aside. Discard bay leaf, flake fish, removing any bones, and set aside. In a large saucepan, melt margarine over low heat. Add onion and cook 5 minutes, stirring occasionally. Stir in flour and cook 1 minute, stirring. Remove pan from heat and gradually stir in reserved milk.

Bring slowly to a boil, stirring, and cook, stirring, until mixture thickens. Add flaked fish, capers, chives, salt and pepper and simmer 5 minutes, stirring. Garnish with basil sprigs and serve with freshly cooked paglia e fieno.

Makes 4-3/4 cups or 6 servings.

Total Cals: 811
Cals per portion: 135
Cals per cup: 171

Total fat: 20.7 g
Fat per portion: 3.5 g
Fat per cup: 4.4 g

CLAM & ZUCCHINI

2 teaspoons sunflower oil
1 bunch green onions, cut into 1/2-inch lengths
1 green bell pepper, sliced
4 oz. mushrooms, sliced
2 zucchini, sliced
1 lb. tomatoes, peeled and finely chopped
1/4 cup dry sherry
1 lb. small fresh clams, scrubbed
Juice of 1 lime
1 tablespoon chopped fresh mixed herbs
Salt and freshly ground pepper
1 tablespoon cornstarch

In a large skillet or wok, heat oil and cook green onions and bell pepper for 5 minutes.

Add mushrooms, zucchini, tomatoes and sherry and mix well. Bring slowly to a boil, reduce heat, cover and simmer 15 minutes, stirring occasionally. Add clams, lime juice, herbs, salt and pepper and mix well. Cover and cook 5 minutes, stirring occasionally. In a small bowl, blend cornstarch with 2 tablespoons water and add to pan.

Cook, stirring, until mixture has thickened, then simmer 3 minutes. Serve with freshly cooked cappellini or spaghetti.

Makes 5-1/2 cups or 6 servings.

Total Cals: 602
Cals per portion: 100
Cals per cup: 109

Total fat: 15.8 g
Fat per portion: 2.6 g
Fat per cup: 2.9 g

Note: Before cooking, discard any cracked or open clams. Once clams have been cooked, discard any unopened ones.

SALMON & TARRAGON

2 tablespoons low-fat margarine
2 leeks, sliced
1 garlic clove, crushed
1/4 cup all-purpose flour
1-1/4 cups low-fat milk
2/3 cup fish or chicken stock
1 (14-oz.) can salmon in water, drained, and flaked
2 tablespoons chopped fresh tarragon
Salt and freshly ground pepper
Tarragon sprigs, to garnish

In a saucepan, melt margarine over low heat. Add leeks and garlic, cover and cook 5 minutes, stirring occasionally.

Stir in flour and cook 1 minute, stirring. Remove pan from heat and gradually stir in milk and stock. Bring slowly to a boil, stirring, and cook, stirring, until mixture thickens.

Add salmon, tarragon, salt and pepper and simmer 5 minutes, stirring occasionally. Garnish with tarragon sprigs and serve with freshly cooked linguine.

Makes 4 cups or 6 servings.

Total Cals: 1005   Total fat: 43.3 g
Cals per portion: 168   Fat per portion: 7.2 g
Cals per cup: 251   Fat per cup: 10.8 g

Variation: Use tuna in water, in place of the salmon.

—SHRIMP & YELLOW PEPPER—

2 yellow bell peppers, halved
1-inch piece fresh ginger root, peeled and finely
  chopped
1 bunch green onions, cut into 1/2-inch lengths
12 oz. cooked, peeled large shrimp
3/4 cup low-fat plain fromage frais
2/3 cup low-fat plain yogurt
2 teaspoons finely grated lemon zest
1 tablespoon chopped fresh chives
1 tablespoon chopped fresh parsley
Salt and freshly ground pepper

Preheat broiler. Place bell peppers on a broiler pan and cook under medium heat until skin blisters.

Place bell peppers in a bowl; cover with plastic wrap and leave to cool. Peel off and discard skins, remove and discard seeds and cores and cut flesh into strips.

Place bell peppers in a large bowl, add ginger, green onions, shrimp, fromage frais, yogurt, lemon zest, chives, parsley, salt and pepper and mix well. Serve with freshly cooked tortiglioni.

Makes 4 cups or 4 servings.

Total Cals: 666   Total fat: 6.3 g
Cals per portion: 167   Fat per portion: 1.6 g
Cals per cup: 167   Fat per cup: 1.6 g

SARDINE & TOMATO

1 garlic clove
1 onion
4 oz. mushrooms
1 teaspoon olive oil
1 (14-oz.) can crushed tomatoes
1 (8-oz.) can crushed tomatoes
2 tablespoons chopped fresh mixed herbs
Salt and freshly ground pepper
3 (4-oz.) cans sardines, rinsed, drained and flaked
Basil leaves, to garnish

Finely chop garlic and slice onion and mushrooms. In a saucepan, heat oil and cook garlic, onion and mushrooms 5 minutes.

Add tomatoes, herbs, salt and pepper and mix well. Bring to a boil, reduce heat, cover and simmer 10 minutes, stirring occasionally.

Add sardines and simmer 2 or 3 minutes or until fish is heated through. Serve with freshly cooked rigatoni.

Makes 4-3/4 cups or 6 servings.

Total Cals: 841
Cals per portion: 140
Cals per cup: 177

Total fat: 41.2 g
Fat per portion: 6.8 g
Fat per cup: 8.7 g

CURRIED MONKFISH

2/3 cup fish or chicken stock, cooled
1/3 cup dry white wine
1 tablespoon lemon juice
1 tablespoon curry powder
1 teaspoon each ground cumin, coriander and ginger
12 oz. monkfish, skinned and cubed
2 teaspoons sunflower oil
1 onion, sliced
1 garlic clove, crushed
1 small red bell pepper, diced
4 oz. mushrooms, sliced
3 stalks celery, sliced, leaves reserved garnish
2 zucchini, sliced
2 small carrots, sliced
1/2 cup raisins
2 apples, cored, quartered and sliced

Place stock, wine, lemon juice, curry powder and spices in a bowl and add fish. Stir gently to coat fish, cover and refrigerate 45 minutes. In a large saucepan, heat oil, add vegetables, cover and cook over low heat 10 minutes, stirring occasionally. Add fish, marinade and raisins and stir gently to mix. Bring to a boil and simmer 10 minutes, stirring occasionally.

Add the apples and cook 5 minutes, stirring occasionally. Garnish with reserved celery leaves and serve with freshly cooked spaghetti or tagliatelle.

Makes 6-3/4 cups or 6 servings.

Total Cals: 1000   Total fat: 19.8 g
Cals per portion: 167   Fat per portion: 3.3 g
Cals per cup: 148   Fat per cup: 2.9 g

Variation: Stir in 2 tablespoons half-and-half just before serving.

──── CREAMY TUNA & LEMON ────

6 oz. frozen green peas
1 (14-oz.) can tuna in water, drained
Finely grated zest and juice of 1 lemon
2 cups low-fat plain fromage frais or yogurt
1/3 cup reduced-calorie mayonnaise
2 tablespoons chopped fresh parsley
Salt and freshly ground pepper
Lemon wedges and lettuce leaves, to garnish

Cook peas in a pan of boiling, salted wate
5 minutes. Drain and leave to cool.

Flake tuna into a bowl. Add lemon zest, lemon juice, fromage frais, mayonnaise, parsley, salt, pepper and cooked peas and mix gently but thoroughly. Chill in refrigerator until ready to serve.

Adjust seasoning just before serving. Garnish with lemon wedges and salad leaves and serve with freshly cooked penne.

Makes 5 cups or 6 servings.

Total Cals: 1027   Total fat: 28.9 g
Cals per portion: 171   Fat per portion: 4.8 g
Cals per cup: 205   Fat per cup: 5.8 g

Variation: Use canned salmon in place of the tuna, and finely grated zest and juice of 1 small orange in place of the lemon.

— COD, GARLIC & ROSEMARY —

2 tablespoons low-fat margarine
3 shallots, finely chopped
3 garlic cloves, crushed
1 green bell pepper, sliced
1/4 cup all-purpose flour
1-1/4 cups fish or chicken stock
2/3 cup dry white wine
2 tablespoons lemon juice
2 teaspoons dried rosemary
1 lb. cod steaks, skinned and cubed
6 oz. frozen broad beans or lima beans
Salt and freshly ground pepper
Rosemary sprigs, to garnish

In a large saucepan, melt margarine over low heat.

Add shallots, garlic and bell pepper and cook 3 minutes, stirring. Add flour and cook 1 minute, stirring. Remove pan from heat and gradually stir in stock, wine and lemon juice. Bring slowly to a boil, stirring, and continue to cook, stirring, until mixture thickens. Preheat oven to 350F (175C).

Add rosemary, cod, broad beans, salt and pepper to saucepan and mix well. Transfer cod mixture to an ovenproof dish, cover and cook in the oven 25 minutes, stirring once. Garnish with rosemary sprigs and serve with freshly cooked tagliatelle.

Makes 5-1/4 cups or 6 servings.

Total Cals: 862   Total fat: 16.8 g
Cals per portion: 144   Fat per portion: 2.8 g
Cals per cup: 164   Fat per cup: 3.2 g

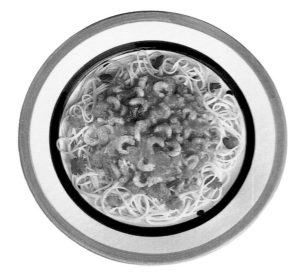

DEVILED SHRIMP

2 teaspoons sunflower oil
1 bunch green onions, cut into 1/2-inch lengths
1 garlic clove, crushed
1-1/2 lbs. tomatoes, peeled and finely chopped
2 tablespoons tomato ketchup
2 teaspoons Dijon mustard
1 teaspoon sugar
1 teaspoon chile powder
1 teaspoon ground cumin
Juice of 1 lemon
Salt and freshly ground pepper
12 oz. cooked, peeled large shrimp
Cilantro leaves, to garnish

In a saucepan, heat oil, add green onions and garlic and cook 5 minutes.

Add tomatoes, tomato ketchup, mustard, sugar, spices, lemon juice, salt and pepper and mix well. Bring to a boil, reduce heat, cover and simmer 10 minutes, stirring occasionally.

Uncover and simmer over higher heat 5 minutes, until sauce has thickened. Add shrimp, mix well and cook 2 or 3 minutes. Garnish with cilantro and serve with freshly cooked linguine.

Makes 4-1/4 cups or 4 servings.

Total Cals: 722
Cals per portion: 181
Cals per cup: 170

Total fat: 23.8 g
Fat per portion: 5.9 g
Fat per cup: 5.6 g

—— SALMON & WATERCRESS ——

1 tablespoon low-fat margarine
2 shallots, finely chopped
1 garlic clove, crushed
6 oz. watercress
3/4 cup low-fat plain fromage frais or yogurt
2/3 cup half-and-half
1 teaspoon Dijon mustard
Salt and freshly ground pepper
2 (8-oz.) cans salmon in water, drained

In a saucepan, melt margarine, add shallots, garlic and watercress, reserving 6 watercress sprigs garnish, and cook 3 minutes.

Leave to cool. Place the cooled watercress mixture in a blender or food processor. Add fromage frais, half-and-half, mustard, salt and pepper and blend until smooth. Transfer to a large bowl.

Flake the salmon, removing any bones, and stir into the watercress mixture. Garnish with the reserved watercress and serve with freshly cooked farfalle.

Makes 4-1/2 cups or 6 servings.

Total Cals: 1166
Cals per portion: 194
Cals per cup: 259

Total fat: 63.5 g
Fat per portion: 10.6 g
Fat per cup: 14.1 g

CLAMS IN WHITE WINE

1 small onion, sliced
1 small carrot, sliced
1 bay leaf
6 black peppercorns
1-1/4 cups dry white wine
2 tablespoons low-fat margarine
2 leeks, diagonally sliced
2 carrots, diagonally sliced
6 oz. button mushrooms
1/4 cup all-purpose flour
2/3 cup fish or chicken stock
1 tablespoon chopped fresh mixed herbs
Salt and freshly ground pepper
1 lb. small fresh clams, scrubbed
Flat-leaf parsley, to garnish

Place onion, carrot, bay leaf, peppercorns and wine in a saucepan and bring to a boil. Remove pan from heat, cover and set aside 20 minutes. Strain wine into a bowl, reserving the wine and discarding vegetables. In a saucepan, melt margarine over low heat. Add leeks, carrots and mushrooms, cover and cook 8 minutes, stirring occasionally. Add flour and cook 1 minute, stirring. Remove from heat and gradually stir in flavored wine and stock.

Bring slowly to a boil, stirring, and cook, stirring, until mixture thickens. Add herbs, salt, pepper and clams and cook 5 minutes, stirring occasionally. Discard any unopened clams. Garnish with flat-leaf parsley and serve with freshly cooked paglia e fieno or tagliatelle.

Makes 6 cups or 6 servings.

Total Cals: 746   Total fat: 15.1 g
Cals per portion: 124   Fat per portion: 2.5 g
Cals per cup: 124   Fat per cup: 2.5 g

—— SMOKED SALMON & DILL ——

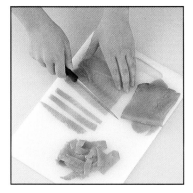

6 oz. smoked salmon
8 oz. low-fat cream cheese
2/3 cup low-fat plain fromage frais or yogurt
3 tablespoons half-and-half
1 small onion, finely chopped
1 tablespoon lemon juice
2 tablespoons chopped fresh dill
Salt and freshly ground pepper
3 tomatoes, peeled and finely chopped
2 stalks celery, finely chopped
Dill sprigs and strips of lemon zest, to garnish

Cut salmon into thin strips and set aside.

Place cream cheese, fromage frais, half-and-half, onion, lemon juice, dill, salt and pepper in a food processor or blender and blend until mixture is smooth. Transfer to a large bowl.

Add smoked salmon, tomatoes and celery and mix lightly. Chill until ready to serve. Adjust seasoning, garnish and serve with freshly cooked pappardelle.

Makes 4 cups or 6 servings.

Total Cals: 775	Total fat: 27.4 g
Cals per portion: 194	Fat per portion: 6.8 g
Cals per cup: 194	Fat per cup: 6.8 g

Variation: Replace the smoked salmon with smoked trout, or salmon or tuna in water.

—— MEDITERRANEAN SHRIMP ——

2 teaspoons olive oil
1 red bell pepper, sliced
1 yellow bell pepper, sliced
2 zucchini, sliced
2 leeks, sliced
3 stalks celery, thinly sliced
2 carrots, diced
2 garlic cloves, crushed
2 beefsteak tomatoes, peeled and finely chopped
2/3 cup fish or chicken stock
1 teaspoon dried oregano
Salt and freshly ground pepper
12 oz. cooked, peeled large shrimp
1 tablespoon chopped fresh basil
Oregano sprigs, to garnish

In a large skillet or wok, heat oil and add bell peppers, zucchini, leeks, celery, carrots and garlic. Cover and cook over low heat 10 minutes, stirring occasionally. Add tomatoes, stock, oregano, salt and pepper and mix well. Cover and cook 10 minutes, stirring occasionally.

Add shrimp, cover and simmer 5 minutes, stirring occasionally. Uncover, increase heat and cook 3 minutes, stirring occasionally, until sauce is thickened. Stir in basil. Garnish with oregano sprigs and serve with freshly cooked garlic and herb tagliatelle.

Makes 5-3/4 cups or 6 servings.

Total Cals: 859   Total fat: 19.9 g
Cals per portion: 143   Fat per portion: 3.3 g
Cals per cup: 149   Fat per cup: 3.5 g

SMOKED TROUT

2/3 cup low-fat milk
12 oz. smoked trout fillets, skinned
2 tablespoons low-fat margarine
1 onion, finely chopped
1/4 cup all-purpose flour
1-1/4 cups fish or chicken stock
3 tomatoes, peeled and finely chopped
1 tablespoon chopped fresh dill
1 tablespoon chopped fresh thyme
Salt and freshly ground pepper
Lemon slices and thyme sprigs, to garnish

Place milk and trout in a large saucepan. Bring slowly to a boil, remove from heat and let stand 20 minutes.

Drain fish, reserving milk. Flake fish, removing any bones, and set aside to cool. In a saucepan, melt margarine over low heat. Add onion and cook 5 minutes. Stir in flour and cook 1 minute, stirring. Remove pan from heat and gradually stir in reserved milk and stock. Bring slowly to a boil, stirring, and continue to cook, stirring, until mixture thickens.

Add flaked fish, tomatoes, herbs, salt and pepper and mix well. Simmer 5 minutes, stirring. Garnish with lemon slices and thyme sprigs and serve with freshly cooked fusilli bucati.

Makes 4 cups or 4 servings.

Total Cals: 858   Total fat: 30.6 g
Cals per portion: 215   Fat per portion: 7.6 g
Cals per cup: 215   Fat per cup: 7.6 g

SALMON & ASPARAGUS

1 lb. fresh salmon fillets, skinned and cubed
Juice of 1 lemon
1 garlic clove, crushed
3/4 cup fish or chicken stock
2 tablespoons dry white wine
1 tablespoon light soy sauce
Salt and freshly ground pepper
2 teaspoons sunflower oil
12 oz. asparagus, cut into 1/2-inch pieces
1 tablespoon cornstarch
1 tablespoon chopped fresh tarragon

In a bowl, mix together salmon, lemon juice, garlic, stock, wine, soy sauce, salt and pepper. Cover, and refrigerate 30 minutes. In a large skillet or wok, heat oil. Remove fish from marinade with a slotted spoon, reserving marinade, and add fish to pan with asparagus. Stir-fry over high heat 2 or 3 minutes until fish is just cooked. Blend cornstarch with marinade and add to pan with tarragon.

Bring to a boil over high heat, stirring continuously, 1 or 2 minutes, until sauce is thickened and glossy. Serve immediately with freshly cooked lasagnette.

Makes 4-1/2 cups or 6 servings.

Total Cals: 1078
Cals per portion: 179
Cals per cup: 239

Total fat: 12.2 g
Fat per portion: 2.0 g
Fat per cup: 2.7 g

TUNA & CORN

1 (14-oz.) can tuna in water, drained
1 (8-oz.) can whole-kernel corn, drained
1 small onion, grated
3/4 cup low-fat plain fromage frais
2/3 cup low-fat plain yogurt
3 tablespoons reduced-calorie mayonnaise
1 tablespoon capers, finely chopped
1 teaspoon Dijon mustard
Salt and freshly ground pepper
1 tablespoon chopped fresh parsley
Parsley sprigs, to garnish

In a large bowl, mix together tuna, corn kernels, onion, fromage frais, yogurt and mayonnaise.

Stir in the capers, mustard, salt, pepper and parsley and mix gently but thoroughly.

Chill in refrigerator until ready to serve. Adjust seasoning, garnish with parsley sprigs and serve with freshly cooked fusilli.

Makes 4-1/2 cups or 6 servings.

Total Cals: 1016	Total fat: 19.7 g
Cals per portion: 169	Fat per portion: 3.3 g
Cals per cup: 226	Fat per cup: 4.4 g

Variation: Place all ingredients except corn in a blender or food processor and blend until smooth. Stir in corn.

SHRIMP & ASPARAGUS

8 oz. fresh asparagus tips
2 tablespoons low-fat margarine
2 shallots, finely chopped
1 garlic clove, crushed
6 oz. mushrooms, sliced
1-inch piece fresh ginger root, peeled and finely
    chopped
1/4 cup all-purpose flour
1-1/4 cups fish or chicken stock
2/3 cup dry white wine
Juice of 1 lime
2 teaspoons light brown sugar
12 oz. cooked, peeled large shrimp
1 tablespoon chopped fresh chives
Salt and freshly ground pepper
Lime slices and chives, to garnish

Cook asparagus tips in a saucepan of boiling
water 3 minutes. Drain well and set aside. In
a saucepan, melt margarine over low heat.
Add shallots, garlic, mushrooms and ginger
and cook 5 minutes, stirring occasionally.
Stir in flour and cook 1 minute, stirring.
Remove pan from heat and gradually stir in
stock and wine. Bring slowly to a boil,
stirring, and continue to cook, stirring, until
mixture thickens.

Add lime juice, sugar, asparagus tips and
shrimp and simmer 5 minutes, stirring. Stir
in chives, salt and pepper and mix well.
Garnish with lime slices and chives and serve
with freshly cooked fiorelli.

Makes 5-1/2 cups or 6 servings.

Total Cals: 764   Total fat: 16.0 g
Cals per portion: 127   Fat per portion: 2.7 g
Cals per cup: 139   Fat per cup: 2.9 g

CHINESE-STYLE FISH

1 (8-oz.) can pineapple chunks in fruit juice
2/3 cup fish or chicken stock
2 tablespoons light soy sauce
2 tablespoons light brown sugar
2 tablespoons dry sherry
2 tablespoons tomato ketchup
1 teaspoon Chinese five-spice powder
1 lb. monkfish, skinned and cubed
2 teaspoons olive oil
1 bunch green onions, cut into 1/2-inch lengths
1 red bell pepper, sliced
1 garlic clove, crushed
1 (8-oz.) can whole-kernel corn, drained
1 tablespoon cornstarch
Salt and freshly ground pepper
Green onions, to garnish

Drain pineapple, reserving juice. Chop pineapple flesh roughly and set aside. Place pineapple juice in a bowl with stock, soy sauce, sugar, sherry, tomato ketchup and five-spice powder. Add monkfish and mix well. Cover, and refrigerate 1 hour. In a large skillet or wok, heat oil. Remove fish from marinade with a slotted spoon, reserving marinade and add fish to pan with green onions, bell pepper and garlic. Stir-fry over high heat 3 to 5 minutes or until fish is just cooked.

Add corn and pineapple and cook 1 minute, stirring. Blend cornstarch with marinade and add to pan with salt and pepper. Bring to a boil over high heat, stirring, 1 or 2 minutes, until sauce is thickened and glossy. Garnish with green onions and serve immediately with freshly cooked tagliatelle.

Makes 5 cups or 6 servings.

Total Cals: 1120
Cals per portion: 187
Cals per cup: 224

Total fat: 15.8 g
Fat per portion: 2.6 g
Fat per cup: 3.2 g

CRAB & WHITE WINE

1 small onion, sliced
1 small carrot, sliced
1/2 stalk celery, sliced
1 bay leaf
6 black peppercorns
1-1/4 cups dry white wine
2 tablespoons low-fat margarine
4 stalks celery, cut into matchstick strips
1 small onion, finely chopped
1/4 cup all-purpose flour
2/3 cup fish or chicken stock
2 (6-oz.) cans crab meat, drained
Salt and freshly ground pepper
2 tablespoons chopped fresh parsley
1/4 cup half-and-half
Parsley, to garnish

Place sliced onion, carrot, celery, bay leaf and peppercorns in a saucepan with wine and bring to a boil. Remove pan from the heat, cover and set aside 20 minutes. Strain wine into a bowl, reserving wine and discarding vegetables. In a saucepan, melt margarine over low heat. Add the celery strips and chopped onion. Cover and cook 10 minutes, stirring occasionally. Stir in flour and cook 1 minute, stirring. Remove pan from heat and gradually stir in flavored wine and stock. Bring slowly to a boil, stirring, and continue to cook, stirring, until the mixture thickens.

Add crab, salt, pepper and parsley and cook 5 minutes, stirring occasionally. Remove pan from heat and stir in half-and-half. Garnish with parsley and serve with freshly cooked spaghetti.

Makes 4-1/2 cups or 4 servings.

Total Cals: 772
Cals per portion: 193
Cals per cup: 172

Total fat: 18.8 g
Fat per portion: 4.7 g
Fat per cup: 4.2 g

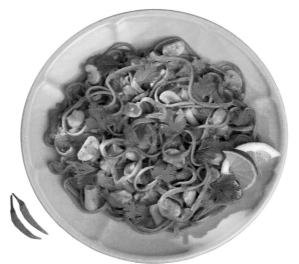

– SPICY TOMATO & MUSHROOM –

1 teaspoon olive oil
1 bunch green onions, cut into 1/2-inch lengths
1 garlic clove, crushed
4 oz. button mushrooms, halved
1 fresh red chile, seeded and finely chopped
1-1/2 lbs. tomatoes, peeled, seeded and finely
    chopped
2/3 cup dry white wine
1 teaspoon ground cumin
Salt and freshly ground pepper
Lemon and lime slices and cilantro leaves, to garnish

In a saucepan, heat oil and cook green onions, garlic, mushrooms and chile 5 minutes, stirring occasionally.

Stir in tomatoes, wine, cumin, salt and pepper, mixing well. Bring to a boil, cover and simmer 15 minutes, stirring occasionally.

Uncover and simmer 10 minutes, until sauce has thickened. Garnish with lemon and lime slices and cilantro leaves and serve with freshly cooked linguine.

Makes 3-1/4 cups or 2 servings.

Total Cals: 322	Total fat: 9.4 g
Cals per portion: 161	Fat per portion: 4.7 g
Cals per cup: 99	Fat per cup: 2.9 g

MUSHROOM & GARLIC

2 tablespoons low-fat margarine
1 onion, finely chopped
4 garlic cloves, crushed
1 lb. mushrooms, sliced
1/4 cup all-purpose flour
3/4 cup low-fat milk
1/2 cup vegetable stock
Salt and freshly ground pepper
2 tablespoons half-and-half
1 tablespoon chopped fresh parsley
Flat-leaf parsley, to garnish

In a large skillet or wok, melt margarine over low heat. Add onion and garlic and cook 5 minutes.

Add mushrooms, cover and cook 8 minutes, stirring occasionally. Stir in flour and cook 1 minute, stirring. Remove pan from heat and gradually stir in milk and stock. Bring slowly to a boil, stirring, and continue to cook, stirring, until mixture thickens.

Add salt and pepper and simmer 3 minutes, stirring. Remove pan from heat and stir in half-and-half and parsley. Garnish with flat-leaf parsley and serve with freshly cooked bucatini.

Makes 4 cups or 4 servings.

Total Cals: 430
Cals per portion: 108
Cals per cup: 108

Total fat: 18.8 g
Fat per portion: 4.7 g
Fat per cup: 4.7 g

──STIR-FRIED VEGETABLES──

1 tablespoon cornstarch
3/4 cup vegetable stock
1/4 cup dry white wine
2 tablespoons light soy sauce
1 tablespoon honey
Juice of 1 lime
1 teaspoon garam masala
Salt and freshly ground pepper
2 teaspoons sunflower oil
1 red onion, sliced
1 yellow bell pepper, sliced
6 oz. broccoli flowerets
4 oz. okra, trimmed and halved
3 carrots, diagonally sliced
4 oz. snow peas
4 oz. bean sprouts

In a bowl, blend cornstarch with stock, wine, soy sauce, honey, lime juice, garam masala, salt and pepper. Set aside. In a large skillet or wok, heat oil. Add onion and bell pepper and stir-fry over high heat 1 minute. Add broccoli, okra and carrots and stir-fry over a medium heat 5 minutes. Add snow peas and bean sprouts and stir-fry 1 minute.

Add the cornstarch mixture and bring to a boil over high heat, stirring continuously, 1 or 2 minutes, until sauce is thickened and glossy. Serve immediately with freshly cooked linguine.

Makes 4-3/4 cups or 4 servings.

Total Cals: 661
Cals per portion: 165
Cals per cup: 139

Total fat: 16.4 g
Fat per portion: 4.1 g
Fat per cup: 3.4 g

—— BROAD BEAN & PARSLEY ——

12 oz. broad beans or lima beans
2 tablespoons low-fat margarine
1/4 cup all-purpose flour
1-1/4 cups low-fat milk
2/3 cup vegetable stock
1 teaspoon mustard powder
Salt and freshly ground pepper
1/4 cup chopped fresh parsley

Cook broad beans in a saucepan of boiling water 10 minutes or until tender. Drain and set aside.

In a saucepan, melt margarine over a low heat. Stir in flour and cook for 1 minute, stirring. Remove pan from heat and gradually stir in milk and stock. Bring slowly to a boil, stirring, and continue to cook, stirring, until mixture thickens.

Add broad beans, mustard powder, salt, pepper and parsley and simmer 5 minutes, stirring. Serve with freshly cooked fusilli bucati.

Makes 3-1/2 cups or 4 servings.

Total Cals: 630
Cals per portion: 157
Cals per cup: 180

Total fat: 19.0 g
Fat per portion: 4.7 g
Fat per cup: 5.4 g

Note: You can use frozen broad beans if fresh ones are not available.

——RED WINE & MUSHROOM——

2 teaspoons olive oil
4 shallots, sliced
3 stalks celery, finely chopped
12 oz. button mushrooms
1 garlic clove, crushed
3/4 cup red wine
1/2 cup vegetable stock
1 tablespoon chopped fresh rosemary
Salt and freshly ground pepper
1 tablespoon cornstarch
Rosemary sprigs, to garnish

In a saucepan, heat oil and add shallots, celery, mushrooms and garlic.

Cover and cook over low heat 10 minutes or until vegetables are soft, stirring occasionally. Add wine, stock, rosemary, salt and pepper and mix well. In a small bowl, blend cornstarch with 2 tablespoons water and add to pan.

Bring mixture to a boil, stirring, and continue to cook, stirring, until mixture thickens. Simmer 3 minutes, stirring occasionally. Garnish with rosemary sprigs and serve with freshly cooked tagliatelle.

Makes 3-3/4 cups or 4 servings.

Total Cals: 375	Total fat: 13.9 g
Cals per portion: 94	Fat per portion: 3.5 g
Cals per cup: 100	Fat per cup: 3.7 g

— CHUNKY VEGETABLE KORMA —

2 teaspoons sunflower oil
2 onions, sliced
2 garlic cloves, crushed
1-inch piece fresh ginger root, peeled and finely
   chopped
1 tablespoon curry powder
1 teaspoon each ground cumin and turmeric
4 carrots, sliced
10 oz. cauliflower flowerets
6 oz. rutabaga, diced
1 small eggplant, diced
1/4 cup raisins
1 tablespoon all-purpose flour
2 cups vegetable stock
Salt and freshly ground pepper
2/3 cup low-fat plain yogurt

In a large saucepan, heat oil and cook onions, garlic and ginger 3 minutes. Add curry powder, cumin and turmeric and cook 1 minute, stirring. Add carrots, cauliflower, rutabaga, eggplant and raisins and cook 5 minutes, stirring. Stir in the flour and cook 1 minute, stirring. Remove pan from heat and gradually stir in stock. Bring slowly to a boil, stirring, and cook, stirring, until mixture thickens. Add salt and pepper and mix well.

Cover and simmer 30 to 45 minutes or until vegetables are tender, stirring occasionally. Remove pan from heat and stir in half of the yogurt. Drizzle with the remaining yogurt and serve with freshly cooked conchiglie.

Makes 6-3/4 cups or 6 servings.

Total Cals: 856
Cals per portion: 143
Cals per cup: 127

Total fat: 21.5 g
Fat per portion: 3.6 g
Fat per cup: 3.2 g

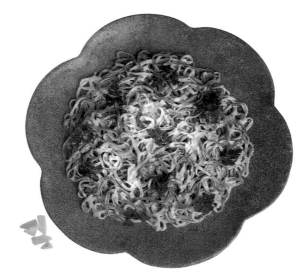

GARLIC & HERB

2 shallots
4 garlic cloves
6 oz. low-fat cream cheese
1 cup low-fat plain fromage frais
2/3 cup half-and-half
3 or 4 tablespoons chopped fresh mixed herbs
Salt and freshly ground pepper
Chervil sprigs, to garnish

Finely chop shallots and crush garlic.

In a bowl, mix together shallots, garlic and cream cheese and mix well. Stir in fromage frais and half-and-half. Stir in mixed herbs, salt and pepper and mix thoroughly. Cover and chill in the refrigerator until ready to serve.

Adjust seasoning, garnish with chervil sprigs and serve with freshly cooked paglia e fieno or spaghetti.

Makes 2-3/4 cups or 4 servings.

Total Cals: 678
Cals per portion: 170
Cals per cup: 246

Total fat: 40.6 g
Fat per portion: 10.1 g
Fat per cup: 14.8 g

Variation: Place all the ingredients in a blender or food processor and blend until smooth, if preferred.

—— THREE PEPPER & TOMATO ——

2 teaspoons olive oil
2 leeks, sliced
2 garlic cloves, crushed
1 red, 1 green and 1 yellow bell pepper, diced
2 zucchini, sliced
1 lb. tomatoes, peeled and chopped
1/3 cup vegetable stock
1/4 cup dry white wine
Salt and freshly ground pepper
2 tablespoons chopped fresh basil
Basil sprigs, to garnish

In a large skillet or wok, heat oil and cook leeks and garlic 5 minutes.

Add bell peppers and zucchini and cook 5 minutes, stirring occasionally. Add tomatoes, stock, wine, salt and pepper and mix well. Bring to a boil, cover and simmer 15 minutes, stirring occasionally.

Stir in basil, garnish with basil sprigs and serve with freshly cooked lasagnette.

Makes 5-1/2 cups or 6 servings.

Total Cals: 450	Total fat: 15.6 g
Cals per portion: 75	Fat per portion: 2.6 g
Cals per cup: 82	Fat per cup: 2.8 g

RATATOUILLE

1 large eggplant, quartered and sliced
2 teaspoons olive oil
2 onions, sliced
2 garlic cloves, crushed
1 red bell pepper, sliced
1 yellow bell pepper, sliced
1 green bell pepper, sliced
4 zucchini, sliced
8 oz. mushrooms, sliced
1 (14-oz.) can crushed tomatoes
2 tablespoons tomato paste
Salt and freshly ground pepper
1 tablespoon chopped fresh basil
1 tablespoon chopped fresh parsley
Basil sprigs, to garnish

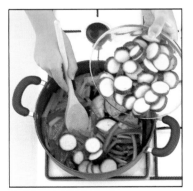

Place eggplant slices on a plate and sprinkle liberally with salt. Leave 30 minutes. Rinse, drain thoroughly and pat dry with paper towels. In a large saucepan, heat oil and cook onions and garlic 5 minutes. Add the remaining ingredients, except the garnish, and mix well.

Bring to a boil, reduce heat, cover and simmer for 30 minutes, stirring occasionally. Uncover the last 10 minutes of cooking time to thicken sauce. Serve with freshly cooked garlic and herb tagliatelle.

Makes 8-1/2 cups or 6 servings.

Total Cals: 608
Cals per portion: 101
Cals per cup: 71

Total fat: 17.9 g
Fat per portion: 2.9 g
Fat per cup: 2.1 g

Note: Sprinkling the eggplant with salt extracts bitter juices.

— CREAMY LEEK & TARRAGON —

3 tablespoons low-fat margarine
3 small leeks, diagonally sliced
1 garlic clove, crushed
1/3 cup all-purpose flour
2-1/2 cups low-fat milk
4 oz. low-fat cream cheese
2 tablespoons chopped fresh tarragon
Salt and freshly ground pepper

In a saucepan, melt margarine over low heat. Add leeks and garlic, cover and cook 8 minutes, stirring occasionally.

Stir in flour and cook 1 minute, stirring. Remove pan from heat and gradually stir in milk. Bring slowly to a boil, stirring, and cook, stirring, until mixture thickens. Simmer 3 minutes, stirring.

Stir in cream cheese, tarragon, salt and pepper and heat gently, stirring. Serve with freshly cooked linguine.

Makes 3-3/4 cups or 4 servings.

Total Cals: 802	Total fat: 36.4 g
Cals per portion: 201	Fat per portion: 9.1 g
Cals per cup: 214	Fat per cup: 9.7 g

— BEAN & LENTIL BOLOGNESE —

1 teaspoon sunflower oil
1 onion, chopped
1 garlic clove, crushed
1 cup green or brown lentils, rinsed
4 carrots, sliced
8 oz. mushrooms, sliced
3 stalks celery, sliced
1 (14-oz.) can crushed tomatoes
2 tablespoons tomato paste
2 cups vegetable stock
1-1/4 cups red wine
1 (15-oz.) can each red kidney beans and cannellini
   beans, rinsed and drained
2 teaspoons dried herbes de Provence
Salt and freshly ground pepper
Flat-leaf parsley, to garnish

In a large saucepan, heat oil and cook the onion and garlic 3 minutes. Add lentils, carrots, mushrooms and celery and cook 5 minutes, stirring. Add tomatoes, tomato paste, stock, wine, beans, herbes de Provence, salt and pepper and mix well.

Bring to a boil, cover and simmer 15 minutes, stirring occasionally. Uncover and simmer 20 to 30 minutes, stirring occasionally, until lentils are tender. Garnish with flat-leaf parsley and serve with freshly cooked spaghetti.

Makes 8-1/2 cups or 6 servings.

Total Cals: 1682	Total fat: 15.3 g
Cals per portion: 280	Fat per portion: 2.6 g
Cals per cup: 198	Fat per cup: 1.8 g

— VEGETABLE & SMOKED TOFU —

1 tablespoon cornstarch
1-1/4 cups vegetable stock
2 tablespoons each dark soy sauce and dry sherry
1 tablespoon tomato paste
1/2 teaspoon each ground bay leaves and cumin
Salt and freshly ground pepper
2 teaspoons sesame oil
1 bunch green onions, cut into 1-inch lengths
2 garlic cloves, crushed
12 oz. smoked tofu, cut into bite-size pieces
1 red bell pepper, diced
1 yellow bell pepper, diced
2 zucchini, diagonally sliced
6 oz. baby corn, halved
3 carrots, cut into matchstick strips
1 (8-oz.) can chickpeas, rinsed and drained

In a bowl, blend cornstarch with stock, soy sauce, sherry, tomato paste, spices, salt and pepper and set aside. In a large skillet or wok, heat oil and stir-fry green onions and garlic over high heat 1 minute. Add tofu, bell peppers, zucchini, baby corn, carrots and chickpeas and stir-fry over medium heat 5 to 8 minutes or until vegetables are just cooked.

Add cornstarch mixture to pan and bring to a boil over high heat, stirring continuously, 1 or 2 minutes, until sauce is thickened and glossy. Serve immediately with freshly cooked fusilli.

Makes 6-1/4 cups or 6 servings.

Total Cals: 1068   Total fat: 36.9 g
Cals per portion: 178   Fat per portion: 6.1 g
Cals per cup: 171   Fat per cup: 5.9 g

— CRISPY SPRING VEGETABLE —

2 teaspoons sunflower oil
1 bunch green onions, cut into 1/2-inch lengths
1 garlic clove, crushed
2 carrots, cut into matchstick strips
1 small red bell pepper, sliced
2 zucchini, cut into matchstick strips
2 oz. spring greens, roughly chopped
4 oz. bean sprouts
4 oz. broccoli flowerets, roughly chopped
1 tablespoon cornstarch
11/4 cups vegetable stock
1/4 cup brandy
2 tablespoons light soy sauce
Salt and freshly ground pepper
Dash of Tabasco sauce
2 tablespoons chopped fresh flat-leaf parsley

In a large skillet or wok, heat oil. Add green onions, garlic, carrots and bell pepper and stir-fry over high heat for 1 minute. Add zucchini, spring greens, bean sprouts and broccoli and stir-fry 5 minutes. In a small bowl, blend cornstarch with stock, brandy and soy sauce.

Add to a pan with salt and pepper and bring to a boil over high heat, stirring continuously, 1 or 2 minutes, until sauce is thickened and glossy. Stir in the Tabasco sauce and parsley and mix well. Serve immediately with freshly cooked linguine.

Makes 4 cups or 4 servings.

Total Cals: 577
Cals per portion: 144
Cals per cup: 144

Total fat: 15.3 g
Fat per portion: 3.8 g
Fat per cup: 3.8 g

TOMATO & RED ONION

1-1/2 lbs. tomatoes, peeled and chopped
2 red onions, sliced
1 garlic clove, crushed
2/3 cup red wine
1/3 cup vegetable stock
2 tablespoons tomato paste
2 tablespoons tomato ketchup
2 tablespoons chopped fresh parsley
Dash of Worcestershire sauce
Salt and freshly ground pepper
Parsley, to garnish

Place tomatoes, onions and garlic in a saucepan and mix well.

Add wine, stock, tomato paste, tomato ketchup, parsley, Worcestershire sauce, salt and pepper and mix well. Bring slowly to a boil, reduce heat, cover and simmer 15 minutes, stirring occasionally.

Uncover and simmer 10 minutes, stirring occasionally, until sauce is thickened. Garnish with parsley and serve with freshly cooked tortiglioni.

Makes 4-1/2 cups or 4 servings.

Total Cals: 384
Cals per portion: 96
Cals per cup: 90

Total fat: 2.8 g
Fat per portion: 0.7 g
Fat per cup: 0.6 g

VEGETABLE CHILE

8 oz. rutabaga, diced
4 carrots, sliced
1 onion, sliced
2 leeks, sliced
1 garlic clove, crushed
1 small red bell pepper, diced
8 oz. baby corn, halved
1 (14-oz.) can crushed tomatoes
2/3 cup vegetable stock
1/4 cup dry white wine
2 tablespoons tomato paste
2 teaspoons hot chile powder
Salt and freshly ground pepper
6 oz. broccoli flowerets
Basil sprigs, to garnish

Place rutabaga, carrots, onion, leeks, garlic, red bell pepper, baby corn and tomatoes in a saucepan and mix well. Add the vegetable stock, wine, tomato paste, chile powder, salt and pepper and mix well.

Bring slowly to a boil, cover and simmer 25 minutes, stirring occasionally. Uncover, add broccoli and simmer 10 minutes, stirring occasionally, until sauce is thickened. Garnish with basil sprigs and serve with freshly cooked fusilli.

Makes 7-3/4 cups or 6 servings.

Total Cals: 595   Total fat: 8.9 g
Cals per portion: 99   Fat per portion: 1.5 g
Cals per cup: 77   Fat per cup: 1.1 g

FRESH GARDEN HERB

1 bunch green onions
1 oz. watercress
1 garlic clove
1-1/4 cups low-fat plain fromage frais
2/3 cup reduced-calorie mayonnaise
2/3 cup low-fat plain yogurt
Juice of 1 lime
1 teaspoon Dijon mustard
1/4 cup chopped fresh mixed herbs
Salt and freshly ground pepper
Lemon and lime slices and watercress, to garnish

Cut green onions into 1/2-inch pieces. Chop watercress and crush the garlic.

Place green onions, watercress and garlic in a large bowl. Add fromage frais, mayonnaise and yogurt and mix well. Stir in lime juice, mustard, herbs, salt and pepper and mix thoroughly.

Cover and chill in the refrigerator until ready to serve. Adjust the seasoning, garnish with lemon and lime slices and watercress and serve with freshly cooked fiorelli.

Makes 3-1/2 cups or 4 servings.

Total Cals: 750
Cals per portion: 187
Cals per cup: 214

Total fat: 45.7 g
Fat per portion: 11.4 g
Fat per cup: 13.0 g

— MUSHROOM, HERB & SHERRY —

2 tablespoons low-fat margarine
1 small onion, finely chopped
8 oz. mushrooms, thinly sliced
8 oz. brown mushrooms, thinly sliced
1/4 cup all-purpose flour
2/3 cup vegetable stock
2/3 cup dry sherry
3 tomatoes, peeled and finely chopped
2 tablespoons chopped fresh mixed herbs
Salt and freshly ground pepper
Parsley sprigs, to garnish

In a skillet, melt margarine over low heat. Add onion and cook 1 minute.

Add mushrooms, cover and cook 8 minutes or until soft, stirring occasionally. Stir in flour and cook 1 minute, stirring. Remove pan from heat and gradually stir in stock and sherry. Bring slowly to a boil, stirring, and cook, stirring, until mixture thickens. Simmer 3 minutes, stirring occasionally.

Add tomatoes, herbs, salt and pepper and heat through. Garnish with parsley sprigs and serve with freshly cooked tagliatelle.

Makes 4-1/4 cups or 4 servings.

Total Cals: 493
Cals per portion: 123
Cals per cup: 116

Total fat: 13.8 g
Fat per portion: 3.4 g
Fat per cup: 3.2 g

CHICKPEA & TOMATO

1 onion
2 garlic cloves
6 oz. button mushrooms
1 (14-oz.) can crushed tomatoes
1 (15-oz.) can chickpeas, rinsed and drained
1/2 cup vegetable stock
2 tablespoons ruby port
1 tablespoon tomato paste
1 teaspoon dried rosemary
1/2 teaspoon cayenne pepper
Salt and freshly ground pepper
Rosemary sprigs, to garnish

Finely chop onion, crush garlic and halve mushrooms.

Place onion, garlic and mushrooms in a large saucepan. Add the tomatoes, chickpeas, stock, port, tomato paste, rosemary, cayenne, salt and pepper and mix well.

Bring to a boil, reduce heat, cover and simmer 30 minutes, stirring occasionally. Garnish with rosemary sprigs and serve with freshly cooked conchiglie.

Makes 4-1/2 cups or 4 servings.

Total Cals: 483	Total fat: 8.9 g
Cals per portion: 121	Fat per portion: 2.2 g
Cals per cup: 107	Fat per cup: 1.9 g

Note: For a thicker sauce, blend 1 tablespoon cornstarch with 2 tablespoons water, add to pan and cook, stirring, 3 minutes.

— SWEET PEPPER & EGGPLANT —

2 eggplant, cut into large cubes
2 red bell peppers, diced
2 yellow bell peppers, diced
2 garlic cloves, crushed
1 bunch green onions, cut into 1/2-inch lengths
3/4 cup tomato juice
1 (8-oz.) can crushed tomatoes
2 tablespoons chopped fresh mixed herbs
Dash of Tabasco sauce
Salt and freshly ground pepper
Oregano leaves, to garnish

Preheat oven to 350F (175C). Place eggplant on a plate and sprinkle liberally with salt.

Leave to stand 30 minutes. Rinse, drain thoroughly and pat dry with paper towels. Place eggplant, bell peppers, garlic and green onions in an ovenproof casserole and mix well. Stir in tomato juice, tomatoes, herbs, Tabasco sauce, salt and pepper.

Cover and cook in oven 45 minutes, stirring occasionally. Garnish with oregano leaves and serve with freshly cooked rigatoni.

Makes 5-1/2 cups or 6 servings.

Total Cals: 391   Total fat: 5.7 g
Cals per portion: 65   Fat per portion: 0.9 g
Cals per cup: 71   Fat per cup: 1.0 g

SPICY MIXED BEAN

2 tablespoons low-fat margarine
2 leeks, sliced
1 garlic clove, crushed
4 carrots, sliced
1 green bell pepper, sliced
1/4 cup all-purpose flour
1-1/4 cups vegetable stock
2/3 cup low-fat milk
1 (15-oz.) can each red kidney beans and chickpeas,
   rinsed and drained
6 oz. frozen broad beans or lima beans
1 teaspoon each ground coriander and cumin
1/2 teaspoon each ground allspice and cayenne
   pepper
Salt and freshly ground pepper
Cilantro, to garnish

In a large saucepan, melt margarine over low heat. Add leeks, garlic, carrots and bell pepper and cook 5 minutes, stirring. Add flour and cook 1 minute, stirring. Remove pan from heat and gradually stir in stock and milk. Bring slowly to a boil, stirring, and cook, stirring, until mixture thickens.

Add kidney beans, chickpeas, broad beans, spices, salt and pepper and mix well. Bring back to a boil, reduce heat, cover and simmer 30 minutes, stirring occasionally. Garnish with cilantro and serve with freshly cooked conchiglie.

Makes 5-3/4 cups or 6 servings.

Total Cals: 1107	Total fat: 26.8 g
Cals per portion: 184	Fat per portion: 4.5 g
Cals per cup: 192	Fat per cup: 4.6 g

ASIAN CABBAGE

1 tablespoon cornstarch
3/4 cup vegetable stock
3 tablespoons dry sherry
3 tablespoons light soy sauce
2 tablespoons white wine vinegar
2 tablespoons light brown sugar
1 teaspoon ground ginger
1 teaspoon ground coriander
Salt and freshly ground pepper
2 teaspoons sunflower oil
8 green onions, cut into 1/2-inch lengths
2 garlic cloves, crushed
1 yellow bell pepper, sliced
1 red bell pepper, sliced
12 oz. red cabbage, shredded
5 oz. bean sprouts

In a small bowl, blend cornstarch with stock, sherry, soy sauce, vinegar, sugar, spices, salt and pepper and set aside. In a large skillet or wok, heat oil and stir-fry green onions, garlic and bell peppers 1 minute over high heat. Add cabbage and stir-fry 3 minutes.

Add bean sprouts and cook 1 minute. Add cornstarch mixture and bring to a boil over high heat, stirring continuously, 1 or 2 minutes, until the sauce is thickened and glossy. Serve immediately with freshly cooked lasagnette.

Makes 4-1/2 cups or 6 servings.

Total Cals: 595	Total fat: 14.4 g
Cals per portion: 99	Fat per portion: 2.4 g
Cals per cup: 132	Fat per cup: 3.2 g

NAPOLETANA

2 teaspoons olive oil
2 garlic cloves, crushed
3 stalks celery, finely chopped
2 lbs. tomatoes, peeled and finely chopped
1 tablespoon tomato paste
1 tablespoon chopped fresh basil
1 teaspoon sugar
1 bay leaf
Salt and freshly ground pepper
Basil sprigs, to garnish
2 tablespoons freshly grated Parmesan cheese

In a saucepan, heat oil and cook garlic and celery 5 minutes.

Add tomatoes, tomato paste, basil, sugar, bay leaf, salt and pepper and mix well. Cover and bring slowly to a boil, stirring, then simmer 10 minutes, stirring occasionally.

Uncover and cook 10 to 15 minutes, stirring occasionally. Remove and discard bay leaf. Garnish with basil sprigs, sprinkle with Parmesan cheese and serve with freshly cooked pappardelle.

Makes 3-1/2 cups or 4 servings.

Total Cals: 451
Cals per portion: 113
Cals per cup: 129

Total fat: 23.3 g
Fat per portion: 5.8 g
Fat per cup: 6.6 g

SUMMER STIR-FRY

1 tablespoon cornstarch
2/3 cup vegetable stock
1/2 cup tomato juice
1/4 cup dry sherry
2 tablespoons each soy sauce and tomato ketchup
1 teaspoon each ground ginger and cumin
2 teaspoons sesame oil
1 onion, sliced
1 red and 1 green bell pepper, sliced
6 oz. baby corn, halved
4 oz. broccoli flowerets
2 carrots, cut into matchstick strips
2 stalks celery, sliced, leaves reserved garnish
1 fresh green chile, seeded and finely chopped
4 oz. snow peas
2 tomatoes, peeled and finely chopped

In a bowl, blend cornstarch with stock, tomato juice, sherry, soy sauce, tomato ketchup, ginger and cumin and set aside. In a large skillet or wok, heat the oil. Add the onion, bell peppers, corn, broccoli, carrots, celery and chile and stir-fry over high heat 3 minutes. Add snow peas and stir-fry 1 minute. Add the cornstarch mixture and bring to a boil over a high heat, stirring continuously, 1 or 2 minutes, until the sauce is thickened and glossy.

Stir in the tomatoes and heat through. Garnish with the reserved celery leaves and serve with freshly cooked linguine.

Makes 6-1/4 cups or 6 servings.

Total Cals: 945
Cals per portion: 157
Cals per cup: 151

Total fat: 16.3 g
Fat per portion: 2.7 g
Fat per cup: 2.6 g

PROVENÇAL VEGETABLE

2 teaspoons olive oil
1 onion, chopped
2 garlic cloves, crushed
2 leeks, sliced
1 (14-oz.) can crushed tomatoes
2/3 cup vegetable stock
8 oz. green beans, halved
8 oz. fresh or frozen broad beans or lima beans
3 carrots, sliced
1 tablespoon each chopped fresh basil and parsley
Salt and freshly ground pepper
4 oz. pitted ripe olives, halved
Flat-leaf parsley, to garnish

In a saucepan, heat oil and cook onion and garlic 3 minutes.

Add leeks, tomatoes, stock, green beans, broad beans, carrots, basil, parsley, salt and pepper and mix well. Bring slowly to a boil, reduce heat, cover and simmer 15 minutes, stirring occasionally.

Uncover and simmer 10 minutes. Add olives and heat through. Garnish with flat-leaf parsley and serve with freshly cooked penne rigate.

Makes 5-3/4 cups or 6 servings.

Total Cals: 705
Cals per portion: 117
Cals per cup: 123

Total fat: 25.7 g
Fat per portion: 4.3 g
Fat per cup: 4.5 g

— SPANISH ONION & MUSHROOM —

2 tablespoons low-fat margarine
2 Spanish onions, sliced
1 garlic clove, crushed
12 oz. mushrooms, sliced
1/4 cup all-purpose flour
3/4 cup vegetable stock
1/2 cup Madeira
2 tablespoons tomato paste
2 teaspoons Dijon mustard
1/2 teaspoon ground bay leaves
Salt and freshly ground pepper
1 tablespoon chopped fresh parsley
Flat-leaf parsley, to garnish

In a saucepan, melt margarine over low heat.

Add onions, garlic and mushrooms, cover and cook 10 minutes, stirring occasionally. Add flour and cook 1 minute, stirring. Remove pan from heat and gradually stir in stock and Madeira. Bring slowly to a boil, stirring, and cook, stirring, until mixture thickens.

Add tomato paste, mustard, ground bay leaves, salt and pepper and simmer 5 minutes, stirring. Stir in parsley. Garnish with flat-leaf parsley and serve with freshly cooked fusilli.

Makes 4-1/4 cups or 4 servings.

Total Cals: 530   Total fat: 13.8 g
Cals per portion: 132   Fat per portion: 3.4 g
Cals per cup: 125   Fat per cup: 3.2 g

BEAN & CORN CHILE

2 teaspoons sunflower oil
2 onions, sliced
2 garlic cloves, crushed
1 or 2 teaspoons hot chile powder
1 teaspoon ground cumin
1 teaspoon ground coriander
3 stalks celery, sliced, leaves reserved garnish
6 oz. mushrooms, sliced
2/3 cup vegetable stock
2 (8-oz.) cans whole-kernel corn, drained
1 (15-oz.) can each borlotti or pinto beans and red
   kidney beans, rinsed and drained
1 (14-oz.) can crushed tomatoes
2 tablespoons tomato paste
Salt and freshly ground pepper

In a large saucepan, heat oil and cook the onions and garlic 5 minutes. Add chile powder, cumin, coriander, celery and mushrooms and cook 5 minutes, stirring occasionally.

Add stock, corn, borlotti or pinto beans, kidney beans, tomatoes, tomato paste, salt and pepper and mix well. Bring slowly to a boil, reduce heat, cover and simmer 30 minutes, stirring occasionally. Garnish with the reserved celery leaves and serve with freshly cooked tagliatelle.

Makes 7-3/4 cups or 6 servings.

Total Cals: 1256
Cals per portion: 209
Cals per cup: 162

Total fat: 23.1 g
Fat per portion: 3.8 g
Fat per cup: 2.9 g

— SWEET & SOUR VEGETABLES —

2 tablespoons cornstarch
2/3 cup vegetable stock, cooled
2/3 cup unsweetened pineapple juice
1/4 cup white wine vinegar
3 tablespoons each tomato ketchup and soy sauce
2 tablespoons each honey and dry sherry
1 teaspoon ground ginger
2 teaspoons sunflower oil
8 oz. pearl onions, quartered
6 oz. baby corn, halved
6 oz. broccoli flowerets
6 oz. button mushrooms
4 stalks celery, sliced
2 carrots, sliced
1 small green bell pepper, diced

In a bowl, blend cornstarch with stock, pineapple juice, vinegar, tomato ketchup, soy sauce, honey, sherry and ginger and set aside. In a large skillet or wok, heat oil and cook onions 5 minutes. Add corn, broccoli, mushrooms, celery, carrots and green bell pepper and stir-fry 6 to 8 minutes.

Place cornstarch mixture in a small saucepan. Bring slowly to a boil, stirring, and continue to cook, stirring, until mixture thickens. Simmer 2 minutes. Pour over vegetables and mix well. Simmer 2 minutes, stirring occasionally. Serve with freshly cooked linguine.

Makes 5-3/4 cups or 6 servings.

Total Cals: 768	Total fat: 15.6 g
Cals per portion: 128	Fat portion: 2.6 g
Cals per cup: 133	Fat per cup: 2.7 g

QUICK SPICED TOMATO

1 onion
4 oz. mushrooms
1 garlic clove
1 (14-oz.) can crushed tomatoes
1/2 cup tomato juice
1/2 cup vegetable stock
1 tablespoon tomato ketchup
2 teaspoons dried mixed herbs
1/2 teaspoon ground cumin
Salt and freshly ground pepper
Basil sprigs, to garnish

Finely chop onion and mushrooms and crush garlic. Place in a pan and add tomatoes, mixing well.

Stir in tomato juice, stock, tomato ketchup, mixed herbs, cumin, salt and pepper and mix well.

Bring slowly to a boil, stirring. Simmer, uncovered, 10 minutes, stirring occasionally. Garnish with basil sprigs and serve with freshly cooked conchiglie.

Makes 3 cups or 2 servings.

Total Cals: 167
Cals per portion: 83
Cals per cup: 56

Total fat: 2.2 g
Fat per portion: 1.1 g
Fat per cup: 0.7 g

GREEN ONION & GARLIC

2 teaspoons olive oil
12 oz. green onions, cut into 1/2-inch lengths
4 garlic cloves, crushed
1/2 fresh red chile, seeded and finely chopped
1 lb. tomatoes, peeled, seeded and finely chopped
1/4 cup dry sherry
Salt and freshly ground pepper
1 tablespoon chopped fresh basil
Lemon slices and green onion strips, to garnish

In a saucepan, heat oil and cook green onions, garlic and chile 5 minutes, stirring occasionally.

Add tomatoes, sherry, salt, pepper and basil and mix well. Bring slowly to a boil, stirring, then cover and simmer 10 minutes, stirring occasionally.

Uncover and simmer 10 minutes, stirring occasionally, until sauce has thickened. Garnish with lemon slices and green onion strips and serve with freshly cooked linguine.

Makes 3-1/4 cups or 3 servings.

Total Cals: 341
Cals per portion: 114
Cals per cup: 105

Total fat: 13.3 g
Fat per portion: 4.4 g
Fat per cup: 4.0 g

——MUSHROOM & RED PEPPER——

1 teaspoon olive oil
3 shallots, chopped
2 garlic cloves, crushed
3 red bell peppers, diced
2/3 cup vegetable stock
1/4 cup dry white wine
1 teaspoon ground coriander
1 teaspoon sugar
1 teaspoon white wine vinegar
Salt and freshly ground pepper
1 tablespoon low-fat margarine
10 oz. brown mushrooms, sliced
Cilantro leaves, to garnish

In a saucepan, heat oil and cook shallots, garlic and bell peppers 5 minutes.

Add stock, wine, coriander, sugar, vinegar, salt and pepper and mix well. Cover and cook 5 minutes until bell peppers are soft. Remove pan from heat and leave to cool. Place mixture in a food processor or blender and blend until smooth. Set aside. In a saucepan, melt margarine over low heat. Add mushrooms, cover and cook 10 minutes, stirring occasionally.

Stir in bell pepper sauce and mix well. Heat gently to warm through. Garnish with cilantro leaves and serve with freshly cooked fusilli.

Makes 4 cups or 4 servings.

Total Cals: 383
Cals per portion: 96
Cals per cup: 96

Total fat: 15.4 g
Fat per portion: 3.8 g
Fat per cup: 3.8 g

CRISP GREEN VEGETABLE

1-1/4 cups low-fat plain fromage frais
1/4 cup reduced-calorie mayonnaise
1/4 cup regular plain yogurt
1 garlic clove, crushed
2 tablespoons chopped fresh mixed herbs
Salt and freshly ground pepper
1 bunch green onions, cut into 1/2-inch lengths
1 green bell pepper, chopped
6 oz. cucumber, halved and sliced
4 oz. sugar snap peas or snow peas, halved
3 oz. small broccoli flowerets
Mint sprigs, to garnish

In a bowl, mix together fromage frais, mayonnaise, yogurt, garlic, herbs, salt and pepper. Add green onions, bell pepper and cucumber and mix well.

Stir in sugar snap peas or snow peas and broccoli, mixing thoroughly. Cover and chill until ready to serve. Adjust seasoning, garnish with mint sprigs and serve with freshly cooked conchiglie.

Makes 4-1/2 cups or 6 servings.

Total Cals: 566	Total fat: 25.4 g
Cals per portion: 94	Fat per portion: 4.2 g
Cals per cup: 126	Fat per cup: 5.6 g

— WILD MUSHROOM & THYME —

1 teaspoon sunflower oil
1 small onion, finely chopped
1 garlic clove, crushed
6 oz. oyster mushrooms, sliced
6 oz. shiitake mushrooms, sliced
3/4 cup vegetable stock
1/4 cup dry sherry
4 tomatoes, peeled and finely chopped
1 tablespoon chopped fresh thyme
Salt and freshly ground pepper
Thyme leaves, to garnish

In a saucepan, heat oil and cook onion and garlic 5 minutes. Add mushrooms, stock and sherry and mix well.

Stir in tomatoes, thyme, salt and pepper and mix well. Bring slowly to a boil, stirring, then cover and simmer 15 minutes, stirring occasionally.

Uncover and simmer 10 minutes, stirring occasionally, until sauce thickens. Garnish with thyme leaves and serve with freshly cooked fiorelli.

Makes 3 cups or 2 servings.

Total Cals: 248
Cals per portion: 124
Cals per cup: 83

Total fat: 7.2 g
Fat per portion: 3.6 g
Fat per cup: 2.4 g

CARROT & ZUCCHINI

2 teaspoons sesame oil
2 leeks, sliced
1 garlic clove, crushed
1 lb. zucchini, sliced
1 lb. carrots, cut into matchstick strips
1-inch piece fresh ginger root, peeled and finely
    chopped
4 oz. dried apricots, chopped
1 tablespoon cornstarch
1-1/4 cups vegetable stock
2 tablespoons dark soy sauce
2 tablespoons dry sherry
Juice of 1 lime
Salt and freshly ground pepper
Chervil sprigs, to garnish

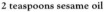

In a large skillet or wok, heat oil. Add leeks, garlic, zucchini, carrots and ginger and stir-fry over high heat 5 minutes. Add apricots and mix well. In a small bowl, blend cornstarch with stock, soy sauce, sherry and lime juice and add to pan with salt and pepper.

Bring to a boil over high heat, stirring continuously, 1 or 2 minutes, until the sauce is thickened and glossy. Garnish with chervil sprigs and serve immediately with freshly cooked penne rigate.

Makes 5-3/4 cups or 6 servings.

Total Cals: 695   Total fat: 15.6 g
Cals per portion: 116   Fat per portion: 2.6 g
Cals per cup: 121   Fat per cup: 2.7 g

—— TOMATO, BASIL & OLIVE ——

1 teaspoon olive oil
2 shallots, finely chopped
1 garlic clove, crushed
1 (14-oz.) can crushed tomatoes
1 (8-oz.) can crushed tomatoes
2/3 cup dry vermouth or dry white wine
2 tablespoons tomato ketchup
Salt and freshly ground pepper
4 oz. pitted ripe olives, halved
3 tablespoons chopped fresh basil
Basil sprigs, to garnish

In a saucepan, heat oil and cook the shallots and garlic 5 minutes.

Add tomatoes, vermouth or wine, tomato ketchup, salt and pepper and mix well. Bring to a boil, reduce heat, cover and simmer 15 minutes, stirring occasionally. Uncover and boil another 5 to 10 minutes, stirring occasionally, until sauce is thickened.

Add olives and basil and mix well. Garnish with basil sprigs and serve with freshly cooked farfalle.

Makes 3-1/4 cups or 3 servings.

Total Cals: 466
Cals per portion: 155
Cals per cup: 143

Total fat: 16.0 g
Fat per portion: 5.3 g
Fat per cup: 4.9 g

RED LENTIL & PARSLEY

2 teaspoons sunflower oil
2 leeks, sliced
1 garlic clove, crushed
2 carrots, thinly sliced
1 red or green bell pepper, diced
6 oz. mushrooms, sliced
1 (14-oz.) can crushed tomatoes
2-1/2 cups vegetable stock
1-1/4 cups split red lentils
Salt and freshly ground pepper
1/4 cup chopped fresh parsley
Parsley sprigs, to garnish

In a large saucepan, heat the oil and cook leeks and garlic 5 minutes.

Add carrots, bell pepper, mushrooms, tomatoes, stock, lentils, salt and pepper and mix well. Bring slowly to a boil, stirring, then cover and simmer 30 to 45 minutes, stirring occasionally, until lentils are cooked.

Add parsley and mix well. Garnish with parsley sprigs and serve with freshly cooked spaghetti or tagliatelle.

Makes 6-3/4 cups or 6 servings.

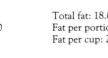

Total Cals: 1318
Cals per portion: 220
Cals per cup: 195

Total fat: 18.0 g
Fat per portion: 3.0 g
Fat per cup: 2.6 g

CHEESE & ONION

2 tablespoons low-fat margarine
1 onion, sliced
1 red onion, sliced
1/4 cup all-purpose flour
1-1/4 cups low-fat milk
2/3 cup vegetable stock
1 tablespoon chopped fresh chives
1-1/2 cups shredded reduced-fat Cheddar cheese
Salt and freshly ground pepper
Chopped fresh chives, to garnish

In a saucepan, melt margarine over low heat. Add onions, cover and cook 10 minutes, stirring occasionally.

Stir in flour and cook 1 minute, stirring. Remove pan from heat and gradually stir in milk and stock. Bring slowly to a boil, stirring, and cook, stirring, until mixture thickens. Simmer 3 minutes.

Remove pan from heat and stir in chives, cheese, salt and pepper, mixing well. Garnish with chopped chives and serve with freshly cooked tagliatelle.

Makes 3-3/4 cups or 4 servings.

Total Cals: 898
Cals per portion: 224
Cals per cup: 239

Total fat: 42.9 g
Fat per portion: 10.7 g
Fat per cup: 11.4 g

EGG & BACON

1 small onion and 1 small carrot, sliced
1/2 stalk celery, sliced
1 bay leaf
6 black peppercorns
1-1/4 cups low-fat milk
2 tablespoons low-fat margarine
2 shallots, finely chopped
3 oz. bacon, diced
1/4 cup all-purpose flour
2/3 cup vegetable stock
3 hard-cooked eggs, chopped
4 tomatoes, peeled and finely chopped
Salt and freshly ground pepper
2 tablespoons half-and-half
1 tablespoon chopped fresh parsley
Flat-leaf parsley, to garnish

Place onion, carrot, celery, bay leaf and peppercorns in a saucepan with the milk and bring slowly to a boil. Remove pan from heat, cover and let stand 20 minutes. Strain milk into a bowl, reserving milk and discarding vegetables. In a saucepan, melt margarine over low heat. Add shallots and bacon, cover and cook 8 minutes, stirring occasionally. Stir in flour and cook 1 minute, stirring. Remove pan from heat and gradually stir in the flavored milk and stock.

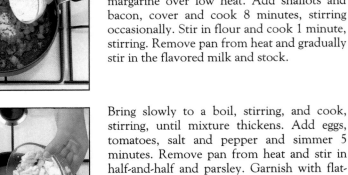

Bring slowly to a boil, stirring, and cook, stirring, until mixture thickens. Add eggs, tomatoes, salt and pepper and simmer 5 minutes. Remove pan from heat and stir in half-and-half and parsley. Garnish with flat-leaf parsley and serve with freshly cooked conchiglie.

Makes 5 cups or 6 servings.

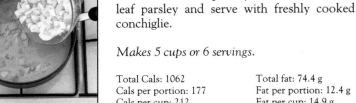

Total Cals: 1062	Total fat: 74.4 g
Cals per portion: 177	Fat per portion: 12.4 g
Cals per cup: 212	Fat per cup: 14.9 g

──CAULIFLOWER & CHEESE──

1 small onion, sliced
1 small carrot, sliced
1 bay leaf
6 black peppercorns
1-1/4 cups low-fat milk
10 oz. small cauliflower flowerets
3 tablespoons low-fat margarine
1/3 cup all-purpose flour
2/3 cup vegetable stock
1 teaspoon mustard powder
Salt and freshly ground pepper
1/2 cup shredded reduced-fat Cheddar cheese
1/2 cup reduced-fat Red Leicester cheese, grated
Cress, to garnish

Place onion, carrot, bay leaf and peppercorns in a saucepan with milk and bring slowly to a boil. Remove pan from heat, cover and let stand 20 minutes. Strain milk into a bowl, reserving milk and discarding vegetables. In a saucepan of boiling water, cook cauliflower flowerets until just tender. Drain and set aside. In a saucepan, melt margarine over low heat. Stir in flour and cook 1 minute, stirring. Remove pan from heat and gradually stir in flavored milk and stock.

Bring slowly to a boil, stirring, and cook, stirring, until mixture thickens. Add the cauliflower, mustard powder, salt and pepper and simmer 5 minutes. Remove from heat and stir in cheese, reserving a little garnish. Garnish with the reserved cheese and cress and serve with freshly cooked bucatini.

Makes 4-3/4 cups or 6 servings.

Total Cals: 872
Cals per portion: 145
Cals per cup: 183

Total fat: 44.3 g
Fat per portion: 7.4 g
Fat per cup: 9.3 g

CHEESE & CUCUMBER

8 oz. low-fat cream cheese
3/4 cup low-fat plain fromage frais
1/4 cup reduced-calorie mayonnaise
4 garlic cloves
1/4 cup chopped fresh mixed herbs
Salt and freshly ground pepper
8 oz. cucumber, quartered and sliced
Lemon slices and tarragon sprigs, to garnish

Place cream cheese, fromage frais and mayonnaise in a food processor or blender.

Crush garlic cloves and add to the blender. Puree mixture until smooth. Transfer mixture to a bowl and add herbs, salt and pepper and mix well. Stir in cucumber, mixing well.

Cover and chill in the refrigerator until ready to serve. Adjust seasoning, garnish with lemon slices and tarragon sprigs and serve with freshly cooked fusilli.

Makes 3-1/2 cups or 4 servings.

Total Cals: 612	Total fat: 31.4 g
Cals per portion: 153	Fat per portion: 7.8 g
Cals per cup: 175	Fat per cup: 8.9 g

CHEESE & BROCCOLI

12 oz. broccoli flowerets
2 tablespoons low-fat margarine
1/4 cup all-purpose flour
2/3 cup low-fat milk
2/3 cup vegetable stock
Salt and freshly ground pepper
4 cup shredded reduced-fat Cheddar cheese

Steam broccoli over a pan of boiling water 4 or 5 minutes, until tender. Leave to cool slightly, then place in a food processor or blender with 1/4 cup water and blend until almost smooth. Set aside.

In a saucepan, melt margarine over a low heat. Stir in flour and cook for 1 minute, stirring. Remove from heat and gradually add milk and stock. Bring slowly to a boil, stirring, and cook, stirring, until the mixture thickens.

Add the broccoli puree, salt and pepper and simmer 5 minutes, stirring. Remove pan from heat and stir in cheese, mixing well. Serve with freshly cooked fiorelli.

Makes 3-3/4 cups or 4 servings.

Total Cals: 664
Cals per portion: 166
Cals per cup: 177

Total fat: 33.3 g
Fat per portion: 8.3 g
Fat per cup: 8.9 g

SMOKED SALMON & EGG

2 eggs
12 oz. low-fat cream cheese
3/4 cup low-fat plain yogurt
2 shallots, finely chopped
1/2 teaspoon paprika
1 tablespoon chopped fresh dill
6 oz. smoked salmon, cut into strips
Salt and freshly ground pepper
Lime slices and flat-leaf parsley, to garnish

Hard-cook eggs in a pan of boiling water 10 minutes. Plunge eggs into cold water and allow to cool. Shell eggs, put into a bowl and mash with a fork.

Put cream cheese, yogurt, shallots, paprika and dill into a bowl and mix thoroughly. Add mashed eggs and stir well.

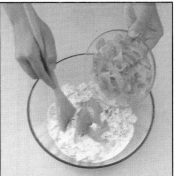

Stir in the smoked salmon, salt and pepper and mix well. Cover and chill until ready to serve. Adjust the seasoning, garnish with lime slices and flat-leaf parsley and serve with freshly cooked tagliatelle.

Makes 4 cups or 6 servings.

Total Cals: 1028	Total fat: 47.2 g
Cals per portion: 171	Fat per portion: 7.8 g
Cals per cup: 257	Fat per cup: 11.8 g

CHEESE, HAM & LEEK

2 tablespoons low-fat margarine
12 oz. leeks, sliced
1/4 cup all-purpose flour
1-1/4 cups vegetable stock
2/3 cup low-fat milk
4 oz. cooked lean smoked ham, trimmed and diced
Salt and freshly ground pepper
1 cup shredded reduced-fat Red Leicester or
   Cheddar cheese
2 tablespoons chopped fresh chives
Rosemary sprigs, to garnish

In a saucepan, melt margarine. Add leeks, cover and cook 10 minutes. Add flour and cook 1 minute, stirring.

Remove pan from heat and gradually stir in stock and milk. Bring slowly to a boil, stirring, and cook, stirring, until mixture thickens. Add ham, salt and pepper and simmer 5 minutes, stirring occasionally.

Remove pan from heat, stir in cheese and chives and mix well. Garnish with rosemary sprigs and serve with freshly cooked tortiglioni.

Makes 4-1/4 cups or 6 servings.

Total Cals: 765
Cals per portion: 127
Cals per cup: 180

Total fat: 37.8 g
Fat per portion: 6.3 g
Fat per cup: 8.9 g

BLUE CHEESE & SAGE

4 stalks celery
1 garlic clove
1/2 cup blue Stilton cheese
1-1/4 cups low-fat plain fromage frais
2/3 cup low-fat plain yogurt
Juice of 1 lemon
1 or 2 tablespoons chopped fresh sage
Salt and freshly ground pepper
Sage leaves, to garnish

Finely chop celery ribs and crush garlic. Crumble Stilton or chop it finely.

Place celery, garlic and Stilton in a large bowl. Add fromage frais and yogurt and mix well. Stir in lemon juice, sage, salt and pepper and mix well. Cover and chill in the refrigerator until ready to serve.

Adjust the seasoning, garnish with sage leaves and serve with freshly cooked linguine.

Makes 3-1/2 cups or 4 servings.

Total Cals: 763
Cals per portion: 191
Cals per cup: 218

Total fat: 43.5 g
Fat per portion: 10.8 g
Fat per cup: 12.4 g

Note: Blue cheese is quite salty, so be careful when seasoning this sauce.

EGG & WATERCRESS

2 tablespoons low-fat margarine
1 small onion, finely chopped
2 garlic cloves, crushed
4 oz. watercress, chopped
1/4 cup all-purpose flour
1-1/4 cups vegetable stock
2/3 cup low-fat milk
3 hard-cooked eggs, finely chopped
Salt and freshly ground pepper
1 tablespoon chopped fresh mixed herbs
Watercress sprigs and celery leaves, to garnish

In a saucepan, melt margarine over low heat. Add onion, garlic and watercress and cook 3 minutes.

Add flour and cook 1 minute, stirring. Remove pan from heat and gradually stir in stock and milk. Bring slowly to a boil, stirring, and cook, stirring, until mixture thickens.

Add eggs, salt, pepper and herbs and simmer 3 minutes, stirring. Garnish with watercress sprigs and celery leaves and serve with freshly cooked penne rigate.

Makes 3-1/2 cups or 6 servings.

Total Cals: 651
Cals per portion: 108
Cals per cup: 186

Total fat: 38.6 g
Fat per portion: 6.4 g
Fat per cup: 11.0 g

—— FETA CHEESE & SPINACH ——

2 lbs. fresh spinach leaves
2 garlic cloves, crushed
2 shallots, finely chopped
Juice of 1/2 lemon
1/4 teaspoon dried thyme
1/4 teaspoon grated nutmeg
Salt and freshly ground pepper
2 cups feta cheese
Oregano leaves, to garnish

Rinse spinach leaves and place in a saucepan. Cover and cook 1 or 2 minutes or until just wilted. Leave to cool. Place spinach in a food processor or blender and puree until smooth.

Add garlic, shallots, lemon juice, thyme, nutmeg, salt and pepper and blend until well combined. Transfer the spinach mixture to a saucepan and bring slowly to a boil. Simmer 5 minutes, stirring.

Crumble feta cheese and stir into sauce just before serving. Garnish with oregano leaves and serve with freshly cooked fusilli.

Makes 3-1/2 cups or 6 servings.

Total Cals: 841	Total fat: 53.8 g
Cals per portion: 140	Fat per portion: 8.9 g
Cals per cup: 240	Fat per cup: 15.4 g

Variation: Use 1 lb. frozen spinach, in place of the fresh spinach. Defrost and puree as with fresh spinach.